Peas, Beans and Greens

Marshall Cavendish London & New York

Edited by Robin Wood

Published by Marshall Cavendish Books Limited
58 Old Compton Street
London W1V 5PA

This material has previously appeared in the Marshall Cavendish
partwork *Grow Your Own*.

First printing 1979

Printed in Great Britain
by Henry Stone and Son Limited
Banbury

ISBN 0 85685 479 4

Introduction

Nothing beats the taste of nutritious greens, freshly-picked from your own garden. Not only do you have the thrill of enjoying the delicious product of your own labour, but there is also the great benefit of substantial savings on the grocery bills. The eight popular vegetables featured in this book will provide year-round mouth-watering goodness—and they are all easy to grow.

Each chapter deals with a single crop, and gives you the detailed and comprehensive instructions you need to grow it to perfection. We begin with the basic facts about the crop—sowing to harvesting time, size and yield—to help you to plan your garden. Three types of symbols, explained below, are used to give an at-a-glance guide to the nature of the crop.

Then we give full details, with clear step-by-step illustrations, on preparing the soil, sowing the crop, caring for it during growth, harvesting and storing, and even preparing your prize products for exhibition.

Of particular value are the separate sections on identifying and combating the pests and diseases that threaten your products, as well as the guides to the most popular varieties available for you to choose from.

Practical both in size and format, *Peas, Beans and Greens* will soon have earned its place on your gardening shelf.

low yield	minimum effort	crops in three months or less
medium yield	needs more care	crops in 4–12 months
high yield	requires special attention	crops in over 12 months

Contents

Peas,
Beans and
Greens

Broad Beans

Vicia faba (fam. *Leguminosae*)
Hardy annual
Sowing to harvesting time: 3-4 months
for spring sowings; 6-7 months for autumn sowings
Size: standard varieties 60-90 cm (2- 3′) tall, dwarf varieties
30 cm (1′) tall
Yield: 5 kg (11 lb) per 3 m (10′) double row

Once an extremely common vegetable, and the only beans grown in Britain—no 'beano' was the same without them— the broad bean is now less widely grown. Nevertheless, the ancient broad bean is an undemanding and rewarding early summer vegetable and is eminently suitable for the amateur gardener. It is the first legume to produce a crop in the early summer, and fresh young broad beans are a welcome change from the winter greens which are the most readily available alternative at that time of the year.

The broad bean is a distinctive plant with a square, erect stem, which can be up to 1 m (3′) tall in most varieties, and is occasionally branched. It is pollinated by insects and bears clusters of white, black-blotched flowers in the axils of the leaves. The fertilized flowers develop into pods which hang down from the leaf axils and, depending on the length of these pods and the number of beans in them, broad beans can be divided into two types. Longpod varieties have the longer pods containing about 8 rather oblong beans; Windsor varieties have shorter pods containing fewer large, circular beans. Longpods are extremely hardy and in most areas can be sown in the late autumn to produce an early crop. Windsor varieties are later, producing a heavy crop of flavoursome beans in summer from a spring sowing.

If you buy broad beans from a shop they are invariably too old and have become hard and unappetizing. Home-grown broad beans, however, can be picked when they are still young and tender—a totally different proposition.

Choosing a site
Broad beans do best on an open site but they are not fussy and will grow quite happily anywhere in most gardens and allotments. You should select your site rather with the interest of other crops in mind. When fully grown the bean will form a hedge up to 1 m (3′) tall which will shade any rows of plants to the south of it. You should make sure that plants on either side get sunshine during at least part of the day by planting the beans so that the rows run north/south. It makes sense, too, to plant the beans alongside a crop, such as lettuce, that will appreciate the shelter the beans provide in early summer; spinach is another crop which benefits from shade in hot weather.

2

Preparing the soil

The best soil for broad beans is a rich heavy loam, well-manured from previous years and deep enough for the plants not to become short of water in the summer. Although broad beans are leguminous plants which obtain nitrogen from the bacteria in their root nodules (and leave the ground richer than they found it) they appreciate additional nitrogen in their early stages. Organic matter also helps by keeping the ground moist during the summer. If the beans can follow on land well-manured from a previous crop, for example summer cauliflower, this is ideal.

Do not worry, however, if your conditions are not perfect. Broad beans will do well on most soils provided that they are not waterlogged. If the beans are to follow another crop directly, just dig the soil well before sowing. If not, the land should be prepared in the autumn. Dig the soil deeply, adding garden compost or well-rotted manure if the soil lacks it—a good general rate is about 4.5 kg per sq m (10 lb per sq yd). For spring sowings leave the ground rough so that it can be better broken up by the frost and add a further light dressing of compost two weeks before sowing.

Broad beans dislike an acid soil so test

Broad beans are an excellent early summer vegetable.

Marshall Cavendish Clay Perry

3

1. Two weeks before sowing add superphosphate at a rate of 60 g per sq m (2 oz per sq yd) and rake in.

2. Use a draw hoe to take out a wide shallow drill 6.5 cm ($2\frac{1}{2}''$) deep and 10 cm (4″) wide.

3. Sow the seeds in a double row with the seeds in one row opposite the gaps in the other.

4. If mice are a problem in your garden place traps at intervals along the row.

your soil and, if acid, add lime as indicated by a soil test kit, about six to eight weeks after digging.

A few days before sowing, add super-phosphate, at the rate of 60 g per sq m (2 oz per sq yd). Rake in the super-phosphate carefully, so as to produce a level seed bed.

Sowing

Broad beans have the biggest seeds of any of the common vegetables, so they can be planted individually just where they are destined to grow. The best method is to prepare shallow drills 6.5 cm ($2\frac{1}{2}''$) deep and 15 cm (6″) wide. Then

place the beans in a double row with one row down each side of the drill. Leave 25 cm (9″) between each bean in a row. Place the beans in one row opposite the gaps in the other row. If you are planting more than one double row, leave a space of 75 cm ($2\frac{1}{2}'$) between each so they do not overshadow one another.

The germination rate of broad beans is low—less than 75%—so sow a few extra plants at the end of the row and transplant them to fill in gaps. Alternatively, if space is limited in a small garden, you can sow two double rows just 10-15 cm (4-6″) apart. As germination is rarely 100%, overcrowd-

4

ing is unlikely to occur. The result of planting like this is a hedge of beans 30-45 cm (1-1½') wide.

Broad bean seeds will germinate at any temperature above freezing and the bright green seed leaves should emerge above ground 1-2 weeks after sowing.

Spring-sown beans

The commonest time to sow beans outdoors is from late winter to early spring depending on local weather conditions. You can plant in the late winter if you have a sheltered garden with a mild climate but should wait until the middle of early spring in colder and more exposed places. The beans from these sowings will be ready for picking from the beginning of early summer. If you want an earlier crop you can sow under cloches, up to a month sooner. Remove the cloches when the plants start to touch the roof.

Broad beans are a cold weather crop and do not do really well during the heat of the summer. Nevertheless, staggered sowings will give you crops throughout the summer. You can sow in mid-spring to pick in late summer and again in early summer for an early autumn crop.

Autumn-sown beans

The hardy broad bean can withstand severe frosts as low as minus 7-9°C (15-20°F) and is thus suitable for autumn sowing in all but the coldest areas. Pick a hardy longpod variety, like *Aquadulce*, and sow in the usual way in late autumn.

There is often little advantage in autumn sowing, however, unless you plan to use the broad beans as wind protection for another crop. Autumn-sown broad beans will crop 2-3 weeks earlier than spring-sown beans and are also less likely to be attacked by bean aphis, but against these advantages there is always the possibility that a cold, wet winter will destroy the crop entirely.

Some gardeners protect autumn-sown beans with cloches but, even if these are available, risks are involved. If the winter is mild the beans will grow so

strongly that they will have to be uncovered in the early spring. A sudden cold spell, once the cloches have been removed, could then kill off all the early growth.

Dwarf beans

If you do have cloches available for broad beans you are better advised to grow a dwarf variety. These plants grow to about 30-45 cm (1-1½') tall, so they are unlikely to become too big too early in the season. They are also useful in a small garden or allotment where there is not room to grow taller varieties. Do not expect such a heavy crop as you would get with taller varieties, however.

Sow a dwarf variety in single rows with 25-30 cm (9-12") between plants and 30-60 cm (1-2') between the rows, depending on the variety. The plants will grow to produce a bush with three to five stems about 45 cm (1½') wide.

Care and cultivation

Broad beans grow at a time when weed growth is particularly strong, so regular hoeing around the plants is necessary, especially when they are small. Additionally some weeds, such as thistles, occasionally grow up within the rows very close to the beans. Do not risk trying to remove these with a hoe. Pull them up by hand.

In a wettish year, broad beans will not need watering, as the early summer soil should still be fairly moist. They cannot withstand drought, however. If the soil does begin to dry out, as it may well do for late crops, water generously.

Although they are not true climbers like runner beans, broad beans are, nevertheless, tallish plants with a good deal of bushy foliage, which is supported by quite shallow root systems, so you will need to give all but dwarf varieties some help against the wind to prevent them being blown down. Small plants can be supported by earthing up for about 7-15 cm (3-6") around the stems (this also gives some protection against very cold or very wet weather for beans

1. Draw soil up round the bases of young plants to give them support and to protect them from the weather.

2. Hoe carefully to remove weeds. Pull up any weeds growing very close to the plants by hand.

3. Broad beans may be blown over in windy weather. Support them with stakes and string.

4. Pick off the growing points to deter bean aphis and to encourage bigger pods.

sown in late autumn, and over-wintered) and by placing twigs in the ground alongside the plants in the same way that you would for peas.

Twigs are not sufficient, however, for tall varieties in windy areas, particularly on sandy soils. In such areas, tie the plants in with string. Place thin stakes or canes at 1 m (3′) intervals down both sides of the double rows close to the beans. Then tie round the stakes with

twine 30 cm (1′) and 60 cm (2′) above the ground. The beans can then lean against this 'pen' in windy weather. As the plants grow, remove the sideshoots from the base of the stems, while they are still small, so that each plant has only one main stem. As soon as each plant has set about four or five flowers, pinch out the growing points at the top of the stems. This has two uses. It encourages the formation of pods and also discourages

5. Immediately after removing the tops spray with derris or bioresmethrin to deter bean aphis.

6. Harvest the beans with a quick downward twist of the hand. The lower pods mature first.

aphids (blackfly) which like to feed on the growing point and youngest leaves.

If the growing points are clean they can be either cooked and eaten like spinach or added to your compost heap. If they are infected with aphids, however, burn them to destroy the pests.

As broad beans are leguminous plants, obtaining nitrogen indirectly from the soil atmosphere through their root nodules, they do not need any feeding once they are growing.

Harvesting

Harvesting broad beans is a matter of taste. If you like mature, hard beans, then leave the pods on the plant until they are beginning to become bronze in colour, before picking. Most people, however, prefer more tender beans. For these, the pods should be picked as soon as sizeable beans can be felt inside. It is a good idea to open one pod, which will indicate if others of the same size are ready. The beans should be a good size but still soft. Alternatively, for a really tender vegetable, try picking very young pods and cooking them, pods and all, as

you would for runner beans.

When you pick your beans, do it by a quick downward movement of the hand.

Aftercare

After the main crop has finished, broad beans often send up suckers which, if left, flower and eventually produce beans. A second crop can be obtained in this way—especially if the old growth is cut out to encourage the suckers. The number of beans which can be collected is normally very small, however, so, unless space is no problem in your garden (in which case you may as well have this little extra crop), cut off the plants at ground level once the first beans are harvested and use the land for something else. Still leave the roots in the soil, though, as the nodules on them contain nitrogenous salts which will help the next crops. Brassicas would be a good follow-up, as they are a leafy crop, needing quite a lot of nitrogen.

If the ground is required immediately for another crop, add the discarded top growth of the bean plants to your compost heap. If not, dig the entire

1. Sow the seeds individually in 10 cm (4′) pots in mid- or late winter. Sow a few more than you actually need.

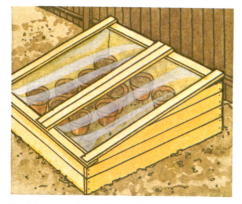

2. After sowing place the pots out in a cold frame or put them on the bench in an unheated greenhouse.

3. The seedlings are ready for planting out in mid-spring. Take care not to damage the root ball.

plants, leaves, roots and stems, well into the soil (chop them up if necessary) and let them rot.

Growing under glass

Broad beans can be successfully sown in pots, either in an unheated glasshouse or in a cold frame, in mid- or late winter and then planted out in early or mid-spring for an early crop. Use one pot for each seed so that the root is disturbed as little as possible when transplanting.

Raising in pots and then planting out is often the only way of getting early broad beans in areas where winters are too severe for autumn planting and the ground is unsuitable to work before late mid-spring.

Exhibition tips

To get really good broad beans for showing, they should be grown on a rich, heavy soil. Add plenty of manure during autumn digging.

You must sacrifice some of the total crop if you wish to grow broad beans for show, since the best beans are produced when only one pod is grown on each cluster. Remove all the pods competing with the one destined for show as soon as the pods have formed. It also helps to grow as many plants as possible, so as to increase your choice when making the final selection.

Select fresh, green, young and well-filled pods without blemishes. They should be large but of a uniform size. The beans inside should be young and tender. Old beans show a black mark on the side, which indicates the point at which the bean germinates; this is considered a blemish.

Broad beans wilt very easily and keeping the beans fresh for show is a problem. Leave picking as late as possible and then store the pods in a damp cloth to reduce transpiration. Sometimes an ugly heel is left on the pod after picking. Remove with a knife.

The normal number of pods exhibited is 18. Simply place them neatly together across a plate or on the bench.

Varieties

The varieties listed here have been separated into Longpod and Windsor types. Nevertheless this classification is rather arbitrary. Modern varieties are often the result of crosses between the two groups and have some of the characteristics of both these groups. Dwarf varieties are separately listed, and all varieties are suitable for freezing.

Longpod

Aquadulce and Aquadulce Claudia: white seeded; hardy early cropper; suitable for autumn sowing; pods 38-45 cm (15-18″) long.

Bunyard's Exhibition Longpod: white-seeded; hardy early cropper; suitable for autumn or spring sowing; well-filled pods about 30-40 cm (12-16″) long; excellent for exhibition.

Imperial White Longpod: white-seeded; spring sowing; long broad pods with up to 9 beans; excellent for exhibition.

Express: green-seeded; spring sowing; very heavy and early cropper; up to 34 pods per plant; excellent flavour, and useful for exhibition work.

Masterpiece Green Longpod: green-seeded; late winter to spring sowing; long pods; excellent for exhibition, very good flavour.

Imperial Green Longpod: green-seeded; spring sowing; heavy cropper; long pods up to 35 cm (14″) long; excellent for exhibition.

Red Epicure: brown-red seeds which become straw-coloured when cooked; spring sowing.

Irish Hardwick

Aquadulce Claudia

Brian Furner

Imperial White Longpod

Brian Furner

Imperial White Windsor

Harry Smith Collection

Imperial Green Windsor

Windsor

Imperial White Windsor: white-seeded; spring sowing; heavy cropper; up to eight beans per pod.

Giant Four-seeded Green Windsor: green-seeded; spring sowing; heavy cropper; short pods, with four or five beans per pod.

Imperial Green Windsor: green-seeded; spring sowing and later; up to seven beans per pod.

Dwarf

The Sutton: white-seeded; suitable for autumn or spring sowing; good as a cloche crop; plants about 30 cm (1') high; pods about 13-15 cm (5-6") long; five seeds per pod but dwarf beans will give smaller crops than the normal-sized varieties.

Harry Smith Collection

Express

Brian Furner

The Sutton

Pests & Diseases

By far the most troublesome pest of broad beans is bean aphis. Happily, however, it is quite easily controlled. If your broad beans escape bean aphis few other pests or diseases are likely to be a serious problem.

Bean aphis: sometimes called black-fly, black aphid, black dolphin aphid, black army, or collier, these tiny insects suck the sap from the plants and also foul the leaf surface with a sticky black substance called honey-dew. The earliest crops are usually unaffected as they produce beans before the aphids have become established, but later crops may be heavily infested.

The aphids congregate particularly on the growing point but are also found on the stem and on the undersides of leaves, which may curl up if badly attacked. Taking out the growing points of the beans reduces the likelihood of attack, but is unlikely to protect the plants completely. Spray or dust the plants with derris or bioresmethrin immediately after removal of the tops. Repeat daily if necessary. The best time to spray is in the evening when bees and other pollinating insects will not be harmed by the spray along with the aphids.

There is some evidence that summer savory discourages attack by the aphids. Try sowing some between the rows of beans.

Chocolate spot: brown spots and streaks on the leaves, stems, petioles, and sometimes also the pods, of the plants are a sure sign of an attack of chocolate spot caused by forms of the fungus botrytis. Good healthy plants, growing on fertile and well-drained soils are never seriously attacked, although autumn-sown plants which have been weakened by frost are susceptible. However, even these plants are likely to recover without treatment. The disease is only serious if the soil lacks either lime or potash and the season is a wet one. The best defence is to plant only in good, well-manured soil, and to space the plants adequately.

Spraying should not be necessary, but Bordeaux mixture or captan can be applied, if the disease becomes troublesome. Destroy infected plants; do not put them on the compost heap.

Bean beetle (Bruchid beetle): These beetles are not a serious threat to a growing crop but rather damage seed which is being stored for future planting. The adults, which look similar to weevils, lay eggs either on the pods of growing plants or on seeds in storage; and the legless and curved grubs which hatch out bore into the seed, feed and pupate inside it. Because of the size of the bean seed, germination is not usually affected but the holes made in the seed reduce the amount of food available to the germinating seedlings, resulting in stunted plants in severe cases. They also expose the seeds to attack by other borers such as millipedes and wireworms, which may be in the soil at sowing time, and to fungal and bacterial diseases.

Seeds containing live grubs or beetles should be burnt to destroy the pest. They should not be placed on a compost heap, as the beatles may spread from it. As the pest is seed-borne the surest precaution against it is to buy seed only from a reputable merchant.

Pea and bean weevil: the same weevil which attacks peas also attacks broad beans. The weevils eat semicircular holes from the edges of young leaves and also eat the nodules on the roots. As soon as this is seen, dust or spray the plants with derris.

Mice: occasionally seed can be correctly sown in good land, and few or no seedlings germinate. This is probably the result of attacks by mice which take the seed and store it. Set traps at intervals along the rows, and inspect the traps frequently.

Royal Horticultural Society, Wisley, Surry

A. A. Turner

Bean aphis is the worst pest of the broad beans. The bean weevil eats small holes in the leaves.

GUIDE TO BROAD BEAN TROUBLES

Symptoms	Probable cause
Small black insects on stems, leaves and growing points; curled-up leaves	Bean aphis
Chocolate-coloured spots on leaves	Chocolate spot
Seed leaves mis-shapen, seedlings stunted, small holes in seed	Bean beetle
Semi-circular holes along leaf edges	Pea and bean weevil
Complete failure to germinate	Mice

Brussels Sprouts

Brassica oleracea gemmifera (fam. *Cruciferae*)
Hardy biennial, usually grown as an **annual**
Sowing to harvesting time: 28-36 weeks
Size: about 90 cm (3′) tall
Yield: 6 plants per 3 m (10′) row, each producing about
1 kg (2 lb) of sprouts

Brussels sprouts—firm, tight, button-like miniature cabbages—are one of the most highly prized of all winter vegetables. These brassicas were practically created for growing in the cool, temperate climates where many other vegetables do not thrive, and they are fairly straightforward to grow. The recent introduction of F_1 hybrids has all but eliminated the once common problem of 'blown' sprouts, those with open and leafy, rather than tight, heads. The flavour of these new varieties is also an improvement, making Brussels sprouts an even more important choice for your garden.

A descendant of the wild cabbage and closely related to Savoy cabbage, Brussels sprouts have a growth habit quite different from other brassicas. The stem of the plant is crowned by a head of inward-curling leaves. From the crown almost down to the base of the stem are closely packed leaf joints, and careful plant breeding has ensured that tight little cabbage-like heads are produced in these joints all the way up the stem. Each of these miniature cabbages is called a sprout. Tradition says that the vegetable originated in the area of northern Europe which is now Belgium, and takes its name from the capital city. It is an economical vegetable to grow, as both the leafy tops and the sprouts make delicious vegetables.

With most brassicas, the buds in the leaf joints do not form until the second season of growth, but Brussels sprouts develop theirs during the first year. The natural tendency of the plant is to form sprouts near the base and then in turn up the stem. After those formed first at the bottom have been picked, the sprouts further up the stem grow bigger, so that a succession of pickings can be made from the same plant. For quite a long time, plants were developed which would produce greater quantities of large sprouts. However, large sprouts have less flavour, and the trend now, started by the commercial growers, is to grow plants which produce a mass of small to

Brussels sprouts—firm, miniature cabbages—are among the most popular winter vegetables.

medium-sized sprouts, all of which come to maturity at about the same time.

It is a good idea to decide what you plan to do with your sprouts before choosing your varieties. For general kitchen use, you will probably want a variety which grows fairly large and produces a succession of sprouts throughout the winter. However, if you plan to freeze most of your crop, choose a commercial growers' variety so that all the sprouts will be ready for harvest and preparation at once. Remember, too, that the picking season can be extended by using a range of varieties which will come into production at different times.

13

The harvesting season for sprouts is from early autumn through to early spring. There are some extra early varieties which will begin to crop in late summer, but, unless you are extremely fond of sprouts, it is rather a waste to begin harvesting them at a time when so many other seasonal vegetables are at their peak.

Brussels sprouts are one of the best cool-climate crops. They are hardy and will withstand considerble frost, although they will not tolerate extreme heat. A hot, dry summer seems to inhibit their capacity to produce tight sprouts in the following autumn. In the initial stages the seeds and young plants need a temperature well above the freezing point, but in the following winter the mature plants will stand quite severe and prolonged frost. The plants will not grow during such extreme conditions, but they will remain alive and will resume growth when the frost is past.

Suitable site and soil

Brussels sprouts are not particular about soil requirements They will grow in almost any type of soil, although they do best in a good deep loam. If the soil is at all acid, correct with an application of lime during the winter, otherwise you may run into trouble with a disease such as club root.

When choosing your site, remember that sprouts can grow into tall plants, and that they will occupy their position for quite a long time. If possible, try to arrange the rows so that the sprouts do not block the sunlight from other crops. A site in full sunlight is not essential, as long as it gets sun for part of the day. And since Brussels sprouts are top-heavy plants, avoid a site which will get the full force of the wind, or be sure to give some wind protection.

Since Brussels sprouts are brassicas, do not plant them in a site previously occupied by another brassica crop, or pests and diseases may build up in the soil. A site last occupied by peas or beans is a good choice. In fact, any position

which was manured for a previous crop is good, but if this is not possible, dig the site deeply and work in a heavy dressing of well-rotted farmyard manure or garden compost, as early as possible in the autumn before planting. This will allow time for the soil to settle and become firm, which is very important if you wish to avoid blown sprouts. If you did not manure the site in the previous autumn, apply a top-dressing of a general compound fertilizer (which has slightly more potash and phosphate than nitrogen in it) at the rate of 90-120 g per sq m (3-4 oz per sq yd), about seven to ten days before planting.

Sowing the seed

Brussels sprouts can be sown in a seed-box, in boxes under cloches or outdoors in a seed-bed and then transplanted to their final positions. Transplanting seems to strengthen the plants and gives an improved crop.

Any available plot of fairly fine soil will do for a seed-bed, as the plants will only be there for a few weeks. Rake the soil over lightly, and make drills about 1.5 cm ($\frac{1}{2}$″) deep, and 15-23 cm (6-9″) apart. For a maincrop of sprouts, sow the seed in mid-spring. Like all brassica seed, that of Brussels sprouts is small and round; sow them quite thinly. Germination should take place within seven to twelve days of sowing, a little longer if the weather is cold. If you have any seed left over, keep it, as it will remain viable for three years.

For sowing in containers, choose standard-sized seed trays or pots filled with a good quality seed compost. Sow as you would for seeds in the open ground, and keep the containers indoors or in an unheated greenhouse.

You can also make sowings in frames or under cloches. Again, follow the instructions for sowing in the open ground. For frame cultivation, water the soil thoroughly before sowing, if it is not already moist, so that further watering is unnecessary during the seedling stage. If sown under frames or cloches, the plants shallow and also widespread, so hand weeding is best. If you do hoe, hoe lightly and shallowly across the surface to avoid damage. If any leaves at the bottom of the plant become yellowed or decayed, remove them immediately, or infection may spread to the sprouts and damage the crops.

If the sprouts are a tall-growing variety, or if they are on a windy site, stake the plants in early autumn, placing the stake on the windward side. Two ties are usually necessary. It also helps if you earth-up round the plants to the level of the lowest leaves at this time. Earthing-up, besides protecting the plants from wind-rock, throws excess moisture away from the stems and gives some protection from frost.

Harvesting

You can encourage the formation and early maturity of sprouts by removing the top 2.5 cm (1″) of growing tip. Do this in late summer or early autumn for maincrop varieties and late autumn for late croppers. This practice, however, tends to decrease the yield. As the crop reaches maturity—28-36 weeks after sowing depending on variety—the lower leaves of the plant will start to yellow. Cut or pull them off—they should come off easily if pulled downward.

Sprouts mature from the bottom of the stem upwards, and should be picked in that order. If you leave sprouts on the bottom of the stem, production of new sprouts further up will be diminished, and the lower sprouts will quickly

HARVESTING

1. As the crop reaches maturity, the lower leaves will start to yellow; cut or pull them off when this happens.

2. Pick sprouts from the bottom of the stem upwards; split sprouts off the stem with a sharp, downward tug.

1. In mid to late winter, sow seeds directly in a cold frame, cover with a thin layer of fine sifted soil.

2. In the greenhouse, sow seeds 1.2 cm ($\frac{1}{2}''$) deep in a seed tray, filled with good quality seed compost.

3. As soon as the seedlings show the first pair of leaves, prick them out from seed boxes into pots or trays.

4. Harden young plants off; place pots in a cold frame outdoors and open light on mild, sunny days.

can be thinned and then left in their original positions to mature if you do not wish to transplant them, but remember that the plants may not be as good in the long run. If the seed is sown outdoors without any protection with glass or plastic, cover with netting at once; birds, especially pigeons and sparrows, are very fond of the plants, both when young and mature.

Another alternative, if you do not wish to take the time and trouble to sow seed and grow seedlings, is to buy plants at the transplanting stage. There are always plenty of Brussels sprout plants available at markets and garden shops in late spring. A delay of a day or two between pulling the plants and replanting them should not cause too much harm.

Planting out

As a general rule, young Brussels sprout plants should remain in the seed-bed, without pricking out, until ready for transplanting. They will need thinning, probably twice, so that they are spaced about 10 cm (4″) apart before moving.

1. Prepare planting holes with a dibber when all danger of frost is past; space plants 45 cm (18″) apart.

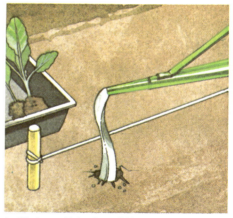

2. If the soil is dry, fill the holes with water; water the seed bed the night before transplanting.

3. Put the plants in carefully, and firm the soil around the roots with a dibber; avoid shallow planting.

4. Test for firm planting by pulling a leaf; it should just tear. If it makes the plant lift up, replant deeper.

Some gardeners transplant most of the crop, but leave a few plants where they were sown, spaced about 45 cm (18″) apart. This can be satisfactory, although those plants left in their original sites will seldom be as good as those which were transplanted, as transplanting benefits Brussels sprouts; the plants grow stronger and produce earlier and better crops.

The time to transplant is when all danger of frost is past, either in late spring or early summer. The plants should be between 10-15 cm (4-6″) high, but not drawn and leggy, with four or five true leaves present. It is essential to allow plenty of space between Brussels sprout plants: allow 75-90 cm (2½-3′) between rows with the greater spacing for the larger varieties, and 45 cm (1½′) between each plant in the row. It is important to plant deeply because the plants are mainly shallow-rooting, and the roots have to support a tall, heavy-headed superstructure. A good rule to follow is to plant with the lower leaves just resting on the soil.

A day just after a heavy rain is the best

Birds, particularly pigeons, can do a great deal of damage; protect plants with netting.

time to transplant. If this is not possible, or in a particularly dry season, water the site thoroughly first. If you can water the seed-bed the night before, so much the better, as the plants will then be well watered. Prepare planting holes with a dibber and fill these with water as well. Put the plants in carefully, to the correct depth, and firm the ground well around them to anchor the roots and encourage the development of tight button sprouts. Do not forget to protect the plants from bird attacks; indeed, it is a good idea to have them netted or in a permanent cage.

Early crops

Early sprouts, ready from late summer onwards, are considered desirable by many gardeners, although this is the time of year when summer vegetables such as runner beans and cauliflowers are both plentiful and cheap.

If you are determined to have early sprouts, then sow in mid- to late winter.

Because sprouts require a long period of growth, and the last frosts sometimes occur in late spring, you will have to sow the seeds under glass. For germination to take place, the temperature of the soil must be 10-13 C (50-55 F); if the winter is mild you can use an unheated greenhouse or conservatory indoors, or sow them outdoors under cloches or frames. If the winter is particularly cold, either delay sowing until the weather warms up and accept that early crops will not be possible, or use a slightly heated greenhouse.

Sow the seed in boxes filled with a good quality seed compost. As soon as the seedlings show the first pair of leaves, they a.e pricked out, or transferred from seed boxes to pots or trays which, like the seed boxes, also need the protection of glass or plastic. The seed boxes, pots or trays should contain a fine soil or potting compost. Transplant the seedlings 5 cm (2″) apart in all directions.

1. Water young plants in dry weather; insufficient watering will result in blowsy, loose, unattractive buttons.

2. In autumn, earth up around the plants to level of lowest leaves, to protect against wind-rock and frost.

If you use trays or pots, you can place them outside the greenhouse, and take the cloches off, or open the frame light, on mild days, to allow the plants to harden off. Plant them into their final positions in early to mid-spring, depending on their degree of maturity. They may continue to need protection at night if the weather is very cold.

To sow the seed directly in a cold frame, prepare the soil by watering it thoroughly so that further watering will not be necessary for some time. Sow the seed thinly in mid- to late winter and cover with 0.3 cm ($\frac{1}{8}''$) of fine soil. Close the light and cover it with a mat until germination has taken place; on warm sunny days, open the frame so that air can circulate around the plants. They will still need protection with the light in periods of heavy rain or extreme cold, particularly if frost threatens at night, when the mat should be replaced also. Thin them to about 10 cm (4″) apart in all directions, and plant them out in mid-spring. Remember your bird protection.

In districts which have a mild winter, the seed is sometimes sown in sheltered borders in autumn and protected by temporary arrangements of glass or plastic against any winter frosts, ready for transplanting in early spring. The main drawback with autumn planting is that autumn-sown plants are much more likely to bolt, or run to seed, without producing sprouts. Also, an unexpectedly cold winter can bring disaster to the whole crop.

Care and development
Remember that sprouts need plenty of water when young, and blowsy, loose buttons often result due to insufficient water at this stage. In hot, dry weather this is particularly important.

A mulch of rotted garden compost or farmyard manure put round the plants about a month after planting will help to keep the soil moist and supply a little more plant food. If you give too much nitrogen while the plants are growing, it will result in blown sprouts later, so any addition of compound fertilizers should be done with caution, and in general only if the soil is very light and quick draining. Avoid sulphate of ammonia and nitrate of soda completely, as they are very rich in nitrates—excessive applications could quickly ruin both taste and quality of your sprouts.

Summer care consists mainly of keeping the surrounding soil free from weeds. Remember, though, that the roots of Brussels sprouts are very shallow and also widespread, so hand weeding is best. If you do hoe, hoe lightly and shallowly across the surface to avoid damage. If any leaves at the bottom of the plant become yellowed or decayed, remove them immediately, or infection may spread to the sprouts and damage the crops.

If the sprouts are a tall-growing variety, or if they are on a windy site, stake the plants in early autumn, placing the stake on the windward side. Two ties are usually necessary. It also helps if you earth-up round the plants to the level of the lowest leaves at this time. Earthing-up, besides protecting the plants from wind-rock, throws excess moisture away from the stems and gives some protection from frost.

Harvesting

You can encourage the formation and early maturity of sprouts by removing the top 2.5 cm (1″) of growing tip. Do this in late summer or early autumn for maincrop varieties and late autumn for late croppers. This practice, however, tends to decrease the yield. As the crop reaches maturity—28-36 weeks after sowing depending on variety—the lower leaves of the plant will start to yellow. Cut or pull them off—they should come off easily if pulled downward.

Sprouts mature from the bottom of the stem upwards, and should be picked in that order. If you leave sprouts on the bottom of the stem, production of new sprouts further up will be diminished, and the lower sprouts will quickly

HARVESTING

1. **As the crop reaches maturity, the lower leaves will start to yellow; cut or pull them off when this happens.**

2. **Pick sprouts from the bottom of the stem upwards; split sprouts off the stem with a sharp, downward tug.**

19

After harvesting is finished, dig up the plants. Burn the roots, to avoid risk of club root disease. Chop up the woody stems with a spade, and put them on the compost heap.

become inedible and subject to infection or infestation by pests.

Begin picking the lower sprouts when they are about 2.5 cm (1″) in diameter, as large sprouts are not nearly as tasty as small ones. Split each sprout off the stem with a sharp, downward tug; if they do not come off easily, use a sharp knife rather than damage the stem by pulling. Spread the harvesting evenly over all the plants; never strip one plant of all sprouts, unless it is to be a once-only harvest, perhaps for freezing.

Once the sprouts towards the top of the stem are well developed, you can cut off the top leafy growth and cook it like cabbage. After the top is cut, the remaining sprouts will mature quite quickly. Otherwise, the top growth can be left on until all the sprouts have been harvested, and will then provide some useful 'greens' in mid-spring. Some gardeners, who want all their sprouts early and small for freezing, cut off the top several weeks before the crop is ready for picking. Most of the sprouts will then mature at the same time.

Care after harvesting

Almost every part of the Brussels sprout plant is used. The sprouts and crown are both eaten, leaving only the stout, woody stem. Some gardeners leave a few stumps of Brussels sprouts in the ground over winter, to produce early spring greens. This is generally a bad idea because the stumps provide a convenient overwintering place for serious brassica pests, such as whitefly and aphids. Having overwintered on the stumps, they then come to life in spring and re-infest newly planted brassica crops.

After harvesting the sprouts and the leafy tops, the best policy is to dig the stumps completely out of the ground. Chop off and burn the root, to avoid the risk of club root. This is why it is much better to dig rather than pull up the stumps. If you pull the stumps out, the root may break off below ground level and remain in the soil to harbour pests and diseases.

The woody stem will rot in time, but should be chopped up with a spade to aid decay. It can be dug into the soil but is probably best incorporated in the compost heap.

A Brussels sprout crop is a heavy drain on soil, which will benefit from a generous manuring before being used again.

Exhibition tips

Brussels sprouts when well grown can make a fine display on the show bench, whether in individual classes or as part of a collection. There are no special cultivation requirements for sprouts intended for showing; good general cultivation should lead to sprouts excellent for both kitchen and show use. They are worth a maximum of fifteen points, and fifty sprouts is the usual number required for both single dishes and collections.

Judges will look for fresh, solid and tightly closed sprouts. As with most vegetables, enormous size is not of paramount importance, and small sprouts which are tightly closed will be favoured over large, loose, blowsy ones.

Try to leave the selection of the sprouts until the last possible moment. Although they will keep for several days when stored in a damp sack in a cool, dark shed or cellar, they really look their best when freshly picked. To ensure that the sprouts are as uniform as possible, it is a good idea to first select one sprout as a control; it should be slightly smaller than average, no more than 3.7 cm (1½″) in diameter and tightly closed. Using this sprout as a reference select about one hundred more. This seems like an extravagant number, but you may need a good supply of replacements at the show bench, and it is better to have a few extra. Although they are tough, strong growers, do not handle the sprouts carelessly, or they may bruise.

Little is needed in the way of preparation. If the tiny leaves at the base of the sprouts look yellow or are otherwise unsightly, cut them off with a sharp knife. Do not pick off too many outer leaves, though, because the inner leaves are paler and less attractive. Then cut all stems to the same length, preferably short.

If the sprouts are being packed for transport to the show, make sure they are packed tightly enough; otherwise, they may bump against each other in transit and some damage may occur. If there is extra space in the box, fill it with tissue paper. The sprouts should not be left in the box too long, or the colour will bleach out and rotting may occur. The sprouts are most attractive when displayed on a wire cone packed with moss.

Pests & Diseases

Cabbage aphids: these insects are most troublesome in hot, dry summers following mild winters. The grey aphids heavily infest the undersides of the leaves of sprouts, which then become curled, blistered and discoloured. Because the eggs of cabbage aphids overwinter on the stumps of old brassicas, the best preventive measure is to dig up and either burn or compost the stems immediately after harvesting. Keep the plants well supplied with water, and for severe attacks, remove the worst affected leaves and sprouts and spray the remainder with derris, bioresmethrin or malathion.

Cabbage root fly: these flies are most active from mid-spring through to early summer. The eggs are deposited on or just below the soil surface next to the stems, and the emerging white legless maggots burrow into the stem, and also eat the roots underground. The first obvious symptoms of cabbage root fly infestation are grey-green, wilted leaves and slow-growing plants, smaller than the others. If pulled out of the ground, the roots will be found to contain the maggots, or they may be in the soil round the roots. A preventive measure is to treat the soil with diazinon granules at the time of planting; also treat the seedbed before sowing if an attack occurred the previous year. Surrounding the stems with a small square of tarred felt on the soil when planting will prevent egg laying. If an infestation occurs, remove and burn damaged plants, as well as the soil around the roots.

Cabbage whitefly: these tiny white moth-like insects feed on the undersides of leaves. They are usually a problem in warm weather, although in mild winters attacks occasionally occur. Besides weakening the plants, they exude honeydew, which encourages the growth of sooty mould; in severe cases, young plants will be destroyed very quickly. Prevent serious damage by spraying with a resmethrin-based insecticide as

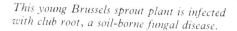

Cabbage aphid damage: infested leaves become curled, blistered, and discoloured.

This young Brussels sprout plant is infected with club root, a soil-borne fungal disease.

soon as you see them. Remove and burn all heavily infested leaves and spray the remainder with a soft soap solution, as an alternative to resmethrin.

Flea beetle: if the leaves of the seedlings and young sprout plants are perforated with numerous small round holes, then there is probably an infestation of flea beetle. These small black insects are most active in fine weather in mid- to late spring but can also be found at intervals throughout the summer. The best preventive measure is to dust the seeds and soil with gamma-HCH; hoeing frequently round the young plants disturbs the soil and discourages the beetles from laying eggs.

Cutworms: these greyish-brown or grey caterpillars feed at night, when they eat through the stems, severing the plant at or slightly below ground level. If your garden is weed-free and well cultivated, you are less likely to have problems with this pest; if an infestation occurs, dust the soil with gamma-HCH.

Cabbage moth/cabbage white butterfly: the green or greyish-brown caterpillars of these insects feed on the leaf tissues of all brassicas, causing widespread damage. The cabbage moth caterpillars usually attack the inner leaves, where they are not easily reached by insecticide. The caterpillars of the butterfly eat the outer leaves, and also foul the remaining foliage with excrement. Both can do a great deal of damage

and ruin the plants completely. As the eggs of both pests are laid on the leaves, remove and destroy any eggs you find on the plant. They will be small and round or conical in shape, light-coloured and laid in batches. If caterpillars do manage to hatch out, hand pick them off in a mild infestation; otherwise, dust or spray the infested plants with derris or a salt solution, 60 g (2 oz) in 4.5 L (1 gal) of water.

Gall weevil: this occasionally attacks Brussels sprouts, although it is more likely on the brassica root crops such as swede. The roots form round hollow swellings in which white maggots will be found, and young plants will be stunted. Remove and destroy badly infected plants; remove only the galls from the remainder.

Club root (finger and toe): this is the most serious disease the home gardener is likely to encounter; it affects all members of the brassica family. It is caused by a fungus in the soil which infects the roots; the symptoms above ground are bluish and wilting leaves, and stunted, slow-growing plants. The roots, when dug up, will be swollen and distorted, black, and rotting, often with an unpleasant odour. Club root is often associated with heavy, badly-drained soils, so a good precaution is to correct any drainage problems before planting. Excessively acid soils also tend to encourage this disease, so correct the soil acidity by liming so that the pH is neutral or slightly alkaline. A further precaution is to sprinkle calomel dust (using pure calomel, rather than the 4% contained in many proprietary brands) before sowing at the rate of 30 g per 1.5 m (1 oz per 5') run. Alternatively, sow the seed in sterilized soil outdoors, or in containers, or in sterilized soil in individual pots. When transplanting, dip the roots in a fungicidal solution of either 60 g (2 oz) pure calomel, or 15 g ($\frac{1}{2}$ oz) of benomyl or thiophanate-methyl to every 0.5 L (1 pt) of water. Because the fungus is soil-borne, if an infection occurs, the site must not be used for brassicas for at least five years—the spores have been known to survive 20 years. All infected plants must be lifted completely and burned immediately.

Wirestem: this fungal infection attacks young plants, causing the base of the stem to become constricted, turn brown and wither. If the plants are not killed outright, they remain stunted and will never fully recover. Seeds or seed-beds dusted with quintozene or thiram or watered with cheshunt compound will usually be free of attacks.

Downy mildew: the symptoms of this fungal infection are white patches on the undersides of the leaves, and yellow speckling on the upper side, followed by wilting. It is often found on seedlings and young plants under glass, or on the outside of the young buttons later in the season. Spraying with zineb will help control downy mildew in mild cases; destroy any plants or buttons severely infected.

Ringspot; a fungal infection, ring spot attacks older plants, and produces round, light brown spots, about 1.3 cm ($\frac{1}{2}$") in diameter on the outer and lower leaves. Infected leaves eventually turn completely yellow and wither. Remove and destroy all infected leaves, and minimize further damage with a light dressing of potash fertilizer.

Grey mould (Botrytis cinerea): this is sometimes a trouble on Brussels sprouts. Infected sprouts become soft, and eventually covered with grey furry mould. Infection occurs through a broken main leaf stalk just below the sprout, and is more likely where too much nitrogen has been supplied. Removal of the affected parts is all that need be done.

Canker: Brussels sprouts may be attacked by this fungal disease, which produces brown or purple spots and cankers on the stems, and results in stunting and sometimes total wilt. Destroy affected plants and do not plant again in the same site.

GUIDE TO BRUSSELS SPROUTS TROUBLES

Symptoms	Probable cause
Leaves turn grey-green and collapse; roots tunnelled, with white maggots inside them	Cabbage root fly
White patches on undersides of leaves of young plants	Downy mildew
Pale brown spots on leaves	Ring spot
Stunted plants with narrowed brown stem bases	Wirestem
Bluish-green, wilting leaves; swollen, black rotting roots	Club root
Stem severed at or slightly below ground level	Cutworms
Small round holes in leaves of seedlings or young plants, or complete defoliation	Flea beetle
Leaves distorted, discoloured; small grey insects on undersides; stickiness on leaves, sometimes black sooty patches	Cabbage aphids
Leaves skeletonized, covered with excrement	Cabbage moth/white butterfly
Soft sprouts, grey fur on outside	Grey mould
Brown or purple spots on stems	Canker
Round swellings on roots	Gall weevil

Varieties

The many F_1 hybrids now available on the market have their drawbacks as well as good points. On the positive side, F_1 hybrids tend to be compact growers, and the stems are tightly covered with buttons. However, the sprouts have been bred to mature all at the same time, and this can be a problem if you do not own a freezer.

The ordinary varieties tend to be taller growing, and, hence, less suitable for small gardens. They are the heaviest croppers, though, and they go on cropping for several months.

Peer Gynt: F_1 hybrid of outstanding quality; dwarf growing and ideal for small gardens; very prolific cropper of uniform, high quality, dark green sprouts; early crops from early autumn.
Achilles: F_1 hybrid; produces high yields of medium-sized sprouts; begins cropping in mid-autumn; can be picked over a long period, as the sprouts do not rot on the stem quickly.
Citadel: F_1 hybrid; firm, tight sprouts; one of the latest croppers; stands well to give sprouts in early spring.
Fasolt: dark green solid sprouts; mid-to late-winter cropping; good flavour and tightly packed.

Peer Gynt

Bedford-Market Rearguard: successful on most soils; very dark green, medium-sized sprouts; will provide continuous supplies from early winter to early spring.
Bedford-Winter Harvest: excellent choice for a mid-season crop; bears medium-sized, dark green, very solid sprouts from mid-autumn to mid-winter.
Cambridge No. 5: prolific cropper of large, high quality sprouts; matures from mid-winter to early spring.
Ashwell's Strain: one of the oldest varieties available; extremely hardy; sprouts can be picked into mid-spring.
Rous Lench: produces small sprouts on fairly short stems; the best variety for an open, windy garden; ready for mid-winter picking.
Perfect Line: F_1 hybrid; mid-season cropper, giving very high yields of medium-sized buttons; slightly earlier that *Citadel;* excellent for early and mid-winter picking.
Bedford-Fillbasket: very large sprouts; harvested from mid-autumn through to early winter; first-class flavour; succeeds on a wide range of soil types.
Roodnerf-Early Button: variety bred for small, deep green sprouts; first-class buttons; excellent for freezing.
Roodnerf-Vremo Inter: early to late

Bedford-Winter Harvest

24

Fasolt

Roodnerf-Vremo Inter

winter harvester; sprouts medium-sized; excellent colour.

Roodnerf-Rollo: uniform, small, solid sprouts; mid-autumn to early winter; heavy cropper.

Roodnerf-Seven Hills: early to late winter variety; small, tight sprouts of good quality.

Focus: F_1 hybrid; new variety with distinctive savoury flavour; sprouts small to medium-sized, dark green, firm; ready for cropping from early autumn through mid-winter.

Lindo: new variety; vigorous and heavy cropper; harvests over a two-month period from early to mid-autumn.

King Arthur: F_1 hybrid; popular mid-season variety, with heavy crop of medium-sized, smooth-skinned sprouts; plants fairly tall, uniform and hardy.

Prince Askold: F_1 hybrid; first-class late variety, with heavy crop of dark green, medium-sized sprouts from mid-winter to early spring; plants of medium height.

Irish Elegance: late autumn to early winter cropper, with good yields of medium-sized, smooth sprouts, plants tall and uniform; sprouts keep well on stem for long period of time.

Early Half Tall (Continuity): medium-sized plants cropping from late summer onwards; large sprouts available until late winter.

Stabilo: medium-sized, firm, dark green sprouts; heavy yielder; sprouts keep well on the stem.

Sigmund: F_1 hybrid; hardy, late maturing variety with smooth, solid, medium-sized sprouts; heavy cropper.

Jade Cross: F_1 hybrid; small dark sprouts, very closely packed; early to late autumn; short-growing; ideal for freezing.

Rubine or *Red:* novelty type which produces red sprouts; very decorative plant; good flavour; ready from late autumn onwards.

Rubine

Cabbages

Brassica oleracea capitata (fam. *Cruciferae*) Savoy cabbages: *Brassica oleracea bullata major* (fam. *Cruciferae*)

Biennial grown as an **annual**

Sowing to harvesting time: 20-35 weeks for red and autumn cabbages; 28 weeks for winter cabbages; 32 weeks for Savoys.

Size: green and red varieties average between 23-45 cm (9-18″) high and 15-60 cm (6-24″) wide; Savoys are about 20 cm (8″) high and 50 cm (20″) wide.

Yield: for red and green cabbages about 10-12 per 3 m (10′) row, each head weighing between 0.5-1.5 kg (1-3 lb); Savoys yield about 6-7 per 3 m (10′) row, each weighing between 1-2 kg (2-4½ lb).

Cabbages are extremely hardy members of the brassica family, thriving in cold, damp winters and capable of withstanding conditions which would destroy many other crops. Their suitability to most temperate climates and soils, and the minimal amount of attention they require, make cabbages one of the easiest crops to grow.

Spring cabbages, sown in summer, are a distinct group and won't be dealt with in this article. Here we look at the types which can be sown from late winter to late spring, for harvesting in summer autumn and winter.

Do not be deterred by the list of pests and diseases that can attack your cabbages; as long as you give your crop reasonable attention it should thrive.

The somewhat unglamorous reputation of cabbage has changed considerably over the last twenty years. Newer varieties are milder tasting than the old strong-flavoured types, and disease resistant varieties have also been bred.

Suitable site and soil

Cabbages will thrive on almost any well-drained ground, but they prefer a medium-light soil which retains a reasonable amount of water. Prepare the soil with lime and apply manure at the rate of one barrow load per square yard (square metre) several months before sowing. If the ground has not been manured, apply a general fertilizer at the rate of 100 g per sq m (3 oz per sq yd) just

1. Prior to sowing, prepare the ground with an application of a suitable compound fertilizer.

2. Prepare the seed-bed just before sowing by raking the soil to a fine consistency. The soil must be dry.

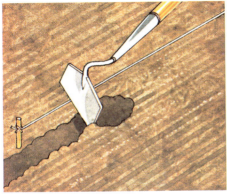

3. Using the side of a draw hoe blade, take out a narrow drill about 2.5 cm (1″) deep and 2.5 cm (1″) wide.

4. Cabbage seeds are large enough to sow individually. Space them in the drill about 8 seeds per 30 cm (1′).

5. When the drill is filled, use a trowel to cover over the seeds with a thin layer of moist soil or peat.

6. When sowing is complete, use the back of a rake to smooth over and firm the surface of the seed-bed.

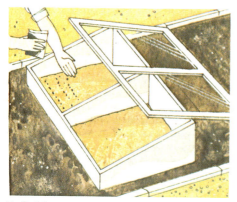

7. Cabbages are ideal for frame cultivation. Prepare the seed-bed and sow as for outdoor cabbages.

8. Sowings can also be made in the greenhouse. Sow in seedboxes filled with a good quality seed compost.

Pat Brindley

Winter cabbages can be sown in growing bags which contain specially prepared compost.

prior to sowing.

Choose an open, sunny site, and remember that cabbages must never follow any other brassicas because of the risk of disease being passed on.

Sowing the seed

Cabbages can be sown outdoors or under glass; the method is the same for both. The time of sowing depends on the variety and on the time you want to

9. When one true cabbage leaf appears, thin the row of young cabbages to about 30 cm (1′) apart.

10. Before transplanting the seedlings, water the ground well using a fine rose on the watering can.

11. To transplant, dig a hole in the moistened ground, fill it with water, and gently place in the young plant.

12. Firm the ground around the transplants, and then water. Continue to water liberally as the plants grow.

13. Keep the cabbage patch free of weeds by hoeing frequently with the blade of a small Dutch hoe.

14. Growing cabbage plants will benefit from an occasional watering with diluted liquid manure.

15. Cabbages are bothered by many insect pests, so an occasional dusting with insecticide will be helpful.

16. As the plants begin to mature, check them frequently and remove any yellowing outer leaves.

17. When the cabbages are ready for harvesting, loosen the soil and lift out the plants, roots intact.

18. Cut off the roots and stem, and remove any coarse outer leaves. Put these on your compost heap.

harvest your cabbages. Plan a succession of sowings from mid spring until early summer for a long period of cutting. Rake the seedbed to a fine tilth and prepare drills 1.5 cm ($\frac{1}{2}$″) deep and 15 cm (6″) apart. Sow at the rate of eight seeds per 30 cm (1′) outdoors.

For a mid to late summer crop, sow the seed thinly in late winter or early spring, in seed beds protected by frames or cloches. Plant into permanent positions in mid to late spring, 30-40 cm (12-15″) apart each way. The bed should be prepared in the same way as for winter crops. Protection may still be necessary if the weather is severe.

Cabbages grown outdoors should be transplanted when four or five cabbage-like leaves have formed.

Care and cultivation

Spring-sown cabbages do not require a great deal of care. Never allow them to dry out, as this will check their growth. Water liberally, especially during hot, dry weather. Hoe around the growing plants frequently to control weeds, to aerate the soil and to deter insect pests from laying eggs near the crop.

Some gardeners sow hyssop, a perennial herb, near the cabbage bed. It is supposed to be a protection against club root disease and to repel the cabbage white butterfly, and many gardeners

Another method of harvesting cabbages is to pull back the outer leaves and cut the heart out.

Leave the stump in the ground. In time new shoots will grow and these can produce greens for cutting.

swear that it works well.

Cabbages are greedy feeders, so during the growing period give applications of dried blood or liquid fertilizer. Top-dressings, particularly nitrate of soda, should never be used on cabbages, as they can give a bad taste to the leaves.

As the plants begin to mature, some of the outside leaves may turn yellow. Break off any yellowing leaves as soon as you see them.

Harvesting and storing

Cabbages are ready for harvesting when the hearts are firm; lift the entire plant with a fork and cut the roots off later, or cut the stem with a sharp knife a little above the base of the lower leaves. Remove the outer leaves, which are much too coarse for eating, and put them on the compost heap.

Mature cabbages in good condition with firm hearts can be kept in a cool airy, frost-proof shed for several weeks. Place the cabbages on a rack made from wood or chicken wire in the shed. Do not stack them on the ground.

Aftercare

Once the cabbages have been cut, the crop is finished and the ground may be cleared. Burn the stems, or chop them up and add them to the compost heap, providing they are free of any pests or diseases. Alternatively, you can leave the stems in the ground overwinter to produce shoots again in the spring and provide another source of spring greens.

Red Cabbage

Red cabbages are usually grown as spring-sown varieties for autmn harvesting. Most people use red cabbage for pickling, but it is also delicious cooked simply and served hot. All red cabbage is round-headed, and all varieties need a longer period for maturing than green spring-sown cabbages. The heads are rather smaller than most green varieties.

To have red cabbages ready for harvesting in autumn, sow the seed in an

Store cabbages on a rack of chicken wire in an airy, frost-free place. They should keep for several weeks.

A healthy row of winter cabbages ready for harvesting.

outdoor seedbed in mid spring, and transplant to a cropping position as soon as four leaves have formed. Water well throughout the growing period, especially if the weather is dry, and follow the cultivation instructions for other cabbages.

The plants are ready for cutting when they are firm-hearted, usually from early autumn. Be sure to cut them before the frost can get to them, as they are not very frost-hardy. They will store for several months in a cool, dry, frost-proof place.

Savoys

Savoys are extremely hardy cabbages with wrinkled, curly leaves. They tend to be rather mild in flavour, and for this reason many people prefer them to other spring-sown varieties. There are many different varieties of Savoys, and the range is wide enough to provide crops ready for harvesting in every month from late autumn to early spring.

However, Savoys should never be grown in a city or in an area of high industrial pollution, since their deeply curled and crinkled leaves trap the soot.

Sow the seed in succession from early spring in a prepared seed-bed. Savoys root less deeply than other cabbages, so they will grow well on less fertile soil and need less fertilizers added. Follow sowing instructions for winter cabbage. The site for final planting should be prepared with a hoed-in application of 60 g per sq m (2 oz per sq yd) of superphosphate and 30 g per sq m (1 oz per sq yd) of potash. Transplant the seedlings when they are large enough to handle and set them out at about 45 cm (18″) apart. Cultivation is the same as for other varieties.

Harvest Savoys when they are firm-hearted. Remove the tough outer leaves and put them on the compost heap. If you want to store some, choose very firm ones and keep them in a cool, airy place. Some varieties will stay fresh for two to three months.

Exhibition tips

If you want to grow cabbages for exhibition, choose your varieties carefully for those suited to your soil and area. Think carefully about the timing of your sowing, so that the cabbages will be in prime condition for your particular show. You do not want your plants to mature too early and become wilted or tough before the event.

It is essential to keep exhibition plants completely free of pests and diseases, so take extra precautions. If the outer leaves become damaged, you can remove these before the damage goes any further, providing this does not make the shape unsymmetrical. The remaining leaves surrounding the heart must be perfect.

Cut the cabbages just before the show, as freshness will count high in the judges' marking. If the cabbages have matured too quickly, lift them completely when they are at their prime and hang them upsidedown in a cool dark place. Spray them with cold water twice a day to prevent wilting.

Three perfectly-matched cabbages should be arranged on a plate at the exhibition hall. The judges will look for cabbages which are fresh and well-shaped with firm tender hearts.

Try hyssop (believed to repel cabbage white butterfly) as a companion plant.

Varieties

Green cabbages

Autumn Pride: F$_1$ hybrid; large, flat heads with very solid hearts; stores well.
Babyhead: small-headed type which produces firm, solid hearts; stores well; good choice for a small garden; sow for summer or autumn cropping.
Celtic: F$_1$ hybrid; extremely winter-hardy; heavy yield; firm, solid heads which store well; mature from early to late winter.
Christmas Drumhead: dwarf, compact and hardy variety well suited to small gardens; matures from mid-autumn; sowings can be made later than most varieties to extend cutting time.
Earliest: very early pointed-head type; sow under glass in late winter or outdoors in early spring for summer and autumn cutting; dwarf growing; excellent flavour.
Emerald Cross: round-headed variety; can be sown in succession throughout spring; high yield; firm, solid heads.
Green Express: new and very successful variety; large heads with crisp, sweet centres; stores very well; sow for summer or autumn maturing.
Golden Acre: popular and reliable; dwarf and compact; suited for small gardens; solid, round heads make excellent salads; matures in summer.
Hidena: F$_1$ hybrid; large, crisp oval-shaped heads; well-flavoured, especially for salads; if lifted with roots, will store for two months; crops in winter.
Hispi: all-year-round cabbage, but will mature in early winter if sown in very late spring; large, conical solid heads with a sweet flavour and crisp texture; compact and good for smaller gardens.
Holland Late Winter White: coleslaw-type cabbage with large, oval heads and crisp, white hearts; matures from late autumn to late winter, depending on sowing time.
Jupiter: new F$_1$ hybrid for harvesting throughout winter months; extremely hardy; large, solid heads; will store for two months.

Christmas Drumhead

Golden Acre

Hispi

Savoy King

Pride of the Market: very large, solid roundhead cabbage; matures early; stores well.

Primo: roundheaded variety; sow in early spring for mid to late summer cutting; small and compact; can be sown close together.

Stonehead: F_1 hybrid; small, compact, round, solid heads; sow close together; sow for summer or autumn crops.

Vienna Babyhead: small but heavy heads with smooth leaves around firm hearts; stores well; matures in summer.

Winnigstadt: very old and reliable favourite; tight, pointed heads with little outside leaf; matures from late summer to late autumn; good for exhibition.

Winter Salad: round, hard, compact heads; very good raw for winter salads; matures late autumn; stores very well.

Red Cabbage

Blood Red: very early-maturing; deep red colour which turns bright red when pickled.

Niggerhead: dwarf red variety; small, round, solid heads which pickle well.

Ruby Ball: F_1 hybrid of outstanding quality; excellent flavour for cooking, salads or pickling; large, solid heads with little wastage; matures in mid-winter and can be harvested for several weeks.

Savoy Cabbage

Alexander's No. 1: largest savoy type; very hardy; firm, dark green heads; cut from mid-winter.

Autumn Green: very dark green heads

Winter Salad

Brian Furner

Niggerhead

Brian Furner

January King

Hurst, Gunson, Cooper, Taber Ltd.

Late Winter White

Brian Furner

with well-curled leaves; matures in mid-autumn for harvesting over several weeks; stores well.

Best of All: large-headed, solid-hearted type matures from late autumn to early winter; excellent flavour.

Dwarf Green Curled: medium-sized, compact and solid heads; very curled dark green leaves; hardy and heavy cropping.

Ice Queen: F$_1$ hybrid; medium to large heads; very hardy; uniform quality; cut from mid-autumn.

January King: hardiest of all spring-sown cabbages; produces large, round, solid heads with a slight red tinge.

January Prince: smaller-headed variety of *January King;* dark green leaves with a reddish tint.

Ormskirk: very hardy savoy which can withstand even the most severe weather; large, solid heads with curled dark green leaves.

Ostara: matures from mid-autumn to mid-winter; uniform curled heads of good quality.

Savoy King: F$_1$ hybrid; one of the most vigorous, uniform-quality and high-yielding varieties; large, round heads with well-flavoured solid hearts; matures in early winter; can survive severe weather.

Winter King: similar to *Ormskirk;* extremely frost-resistant; large heads.

Wirosa: F$_1$ hybrid of *Ormskirk* type; hardy; good colour and flavour; round heads with finely-curled leaves; matures from mid to late winter.

Pests & Diseases

Cabbage aphis: this is a grey or grey-blue aphid which infests the undersides of leaves, from mid-spring through to winter. The eggs will overwinter in the stems. Treat by spraying with derris or malathion.

Cabbage root fly: Spring-sown cabbages are particularly at risk because the flies are most active in mid-spring to early summer. The adults lay their eggs against the cabbage stems, and the maggots hatch and burrow into the stem and devour the roots. The cabbages wilt and die. Lift and destroy any infested plants. An attack can be prevented by dusting the ground with diazinon at the time of planting and again about two weeks later.

Cabbage white butterfly: cabbages in the ground in summer and autumn are liable to attacks by the caterpillars of the cabbage white butterfly. The adults lay eggs on the cabbage leaves, and the caterpillars hatch out and rapidly devour the plants. If unchecked they can destroy an entire crop. Do not wait until the caterpillars are seen to take action. If you see any butterflies, spray the plants with a non-poisonous insecticide such as derris or malathion. Check the cabbage leaves for any yellowish, oval eggs, and remove and destroy them. Should you see any of the yellow-striped green caterpillars, remove them by hand and spray the plants again.

Cabbage moth: Moth larvae can also attack. The moths are nocturnal and rarely seen, so be on the look out for their large, round eggs, laid from mid-spring to mid-summer. The smooth green caterpillars hatch out and burrow into the hearts of the cabbages, destroying them. Remove any eggs by hand, and spray the plants with derris or malathion. Remove and destroy any caterpillars that hatch.

Cabbage white fly: this pest attacks all members of the cabbage family. It is usually a problem during warm weather, although attacks during mid-winter are not unknown. The females lay their eggs on the undersides of leaves, and the flat, scale-like larvae remain attached to the leaves. The secretions of the larvae encourage the formation of sooty moulds, and the cabbages are very quickly destroyed. Prevent a whitefly attack by spraying with a resmethrin-based insecticide at the first sign of the insects. Remove and burn any infested leaves, and spray the undersides of the remaining leaves with a soft soap solution.

Flea beetle: colonies of small, black flea beetles can decimate seedlings and young plants by biting small round holes in the leaves. The crop can be completely destroyed before it has even started to grow. To prevent an attack, dust the leaves of young plants with derris. Hoe

Holes in a head of cabbage caused by the caterpillars of the cabbage white butterfly.

Adults and larva of the cabbage white fly. Eggs are laid on the undersides of leaves.

36

GUIDE TO CABBAGE TROUBLES

Symptom	Probable Cause
Maggots in stems	Cabbage root fly
Holes in leaves	Cabbage white butterfly caterpillar
	Cabbage moth caterpillar, Flea Beetle
White larva on undersides of	Cabbage Whitefly, Club root
leaves, distorted roots	
Wilting leaves	Cabbage root fly, Club root
Rotting stems on seedlings	Wirestem
Brown spots on leaves	Ring spot
White fungus on undersides of leaves	Downy mildew

frequently around the plants to disturb the beetles and stop egg-laying.

Club root (finger and toe): this is the most serious cabbage disease the home grower is likely to encounter. It is caused by a fungus which infects the roots. The first signs of infection are wilting,

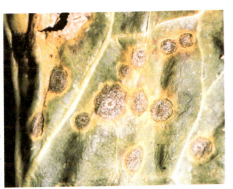

Round brown spots and yellowing leaves caused by the fungus infection ring spot.

Young cabbage plants which have been badly infected by the disease club root.

blueish leaves and dying plants. The roots are swollen and distorted so that they have a club-like appearance. This occurs most frequently on heavy soils which have not been sufficiently limed, so lime the soil before sowing to make it slightly alkaline. Attacks also occur on wet, badly drained soils, so be sure that drainage is sufficient before planting. Dusting the seed-bed and planting holes with calomel dust is another useful precaution and cabbage transplants can be protected by dipping their roots in water containing benomyl, just before planting. The fungus is soil-borne so if an infection occurs remove and burn all plants and do not use the site for brassicas for five years.

Wirestem: Wirestem fungus attacks the seedlings, causing the bases of the stems to turn brown and wither. The seedlings either die or grow into poor, stunted plants. Wirestem can usually be avoided by sowing the seed in slightly alkaline soil or in sterilized compost.

Ring spot: this is a fungus disease which attacks older plants and produces round brown spots about 1.5 cm ($\frac{1}{2}''$) in diameter on the leaves. The infected outer leaves turn yellow, and the inner leaves will also gradually become infected. Remove any diseased leaves as soon as you see them, and prevent further infections with a light dressing of potash fertilizer to harden the growth.

Downy mildew: this disease appears as patches of white fungus on the undersides of the plants. Destroy affected plants.

Ministry of Agriculture, Fisheries & Food

Brian Furner

French Beans

Phaseolus vulgaris (fam. *Leguminosae*) also known as snap bean and string bean
Half-hardy annual
Sowing to harvesting time: 10-12 weeks
Size: dwarf varieties 15-25 cm (6-10″) high, 10-15 cm (4-6″) across; climbing varieties up to 1.8 m (6′) high.
Yield: 9 kg (20 lb) per 10 m (30′) row for dwarf varieties; 13.5 kg (30 lb) for climbing varieties; 1 kg (2 lb) as dried haricots.

French beans make an ideal crop for the home grower; the plants are compact, require little attention, and the yield of succulent, delicately flavoured pods is high compared to the small amount of space needed. Except for protecting early and late sowings from frost damage, little is needed in the way of cultivation, and the plants for the most part take care of themselves. Once they are growing well, the large, attractive leaves form a dense canopy which acts as a weed suppressor. The thick foliage completely shades the soil beneath, and weeds, starved of sunlight, are unable to compete. French beans will crop well in spite of long periods of drought, although heavier crops will result if they are watered regularly in dry conditions. As an additional bonus, the leaves, white or lilac-tinted flowers, and pods, coloured purple or scarlet in some varieties, are exceedingly decorative, and a few plants will enhance any border.

There are both dwarf and climbing varieties available. The dwarf, or 'bush', type, grows 15-25 cm (6-10″) high, while the climbing varieties can be up to 1.8 m (6′) tall; these have growing habits similar to runner beans and will need some form of support. The pods of both dwarf and climbing varieties are 7.5-15 cm (3-6″) long and hang beneath the leaves. There is one exception: the new variety *Remus* carries its pods well above the leaves, for easy picking and early ripening.

Although most varieties have green pods, some are indigo blue, or mottled red and white. French beans with pale yellow pods are called 'waxpod', or 'butter' beans, and are thought by many to have the finest flavour of all. The pods of French beans are round in section, not flat as runner beans are.

Because French beans are only half-hardy in cool temperate climates, they are normally cropped outdoors from

Succulent French beans ready for harvesting; outdoors, cropping begins in mid-summer.

mid-summer through to mid-autumn. By successional sowing, and by giving cloche protection, you can extend the cropping period by a good two months, from early summer through to late autumn. If you have a heated greenhouse available and grow them entirely under glass, then cropping can begin as early as mid-spring.

The beans can be harvested at various stages of development. When the pods are very young and delicate, they are picked for cooking whole. When slightly larger and more mature, the pods are harvested and cut up into pieces before cooking. If left to grow on, the beans inside the pod will begin to swell. These beans are then shelled, and served when green as 'flageolots', or allowed to grow to full maturity, and then dried for winter use as 'haricots'. As a general rule, the more French beans you pick, the heavier the crops will be, as frequent picking encourages the development of more pods.

Suitable site and soil

French beans do best in a sunny, sheltered situation. They will grow in almost any soil, but prefer one that is not too heavy. A heavy soil can be lightened by working in peat, garden compost or coarse sand.

Ideally, you should grow French

39

beans on a plot well manured for a previous crop, such as spinach. If you have no such site available, dig in manure in the autumn before planting, at the rate of one bucketful per sq m (sq yd). The soil pH should be 7.0-8.0. Test your soil some months before planting, and correct if necessary with the addition of lime, (see Improving Your Soil).

This crop does especially well if potassium and phosphorus are given as base dressings, so a fortnight before sowing or planting out, dress with sulphate of potash, at the rate of 15 g per sq m ($\frac{1}{2}$ oz per sq yd), and super-phosphate at 30 g per sq m (1 oz per sq yd) and fork in well.

Sowing

Theoretically, French beans can be sown outdoors from early spring, with fort-nightly successional sowings right th-rough late summer, for late autumn cropping. However, germination will not take place unless there is a minimum temperature of 16°C (60°F), and bean seeds planted in cold wet soil will quickly rot. Secondly, because the plants are sub-tropical in origin, they cannot tolerate even one degree of frost, so early and late sowings will need cloche protection if they are to be at all successful. Local weather conditions are a major factor, and the last frost date varies from year to year and place to place. A basic understanding of the plants' temperature requirements will help you to avoid disappointment, and you can select the right sowing time for your particular garden.

Generally, for early summer crops, sow under cloches in early spring; keep the plants under cloches until the beginning of summer. Main crops can be sown outdoors from mid-spring on-wards, given cloche protection for about a fortnight. French beans which are not given cloche protection should be sown in late spring, or early summer if the site is cold or exposed. Beans grown for drying as haricots should not be sown later than the beginning of summer, as they need plenty of time for proper ripening.

The seeds vary enormously in size, shape and colour, according to the variety selected, but even the smallest are easy to handle and can be sown individually. Because the success rate of germination is relatively low (75%), it is best to sow the seeds in pairs; if both germinate, cut the top off the weaker seedling when the first true leaves appear.

The distance between seeds and rows of seeds varies according to the time of year planted, the planting position, and harvesting requirements. Whatever the planting spacings, make sure the soil has been worked to a very fine tilth. If there are stones or rough lumps of soil, the emerging seedlings will be stunted or mis-shapen. Drills for French beans should be 5 cm (2") deep. If you are growing the beans against a wall or fence, then only one row of plants is needed. Otherwise, sow the seeds in double rows, 30 cm (1') apart. If you have more than one double row, leave 60-90 cm (2-3') between them, so that you can cultivate and pick the crops easily. However, if you are planting French beans for drying as haricots, the rows need only 30 cm (1') between them. This is because the haricot beans are usually harvested all at once, so easy access to every plant is unnecessary.

Sow the seeds at 15 cm (6") intervals for early crops and haricots, and 22 cm (9") intervals for main crops. Germination should take place between 10 days and three weeks after sowing. It is not necessary to water the beans while they are germinating and they should never be soaked before sowing. A word of advice: never leave unused beans on the surface of the soil, or birds will immediately be attracted to the site and quickly peck up the beans. If you have been troubled by birds in past years, it is a good idea to protect the seeds and seedlings with wire mesh netting, similar to that used for peas.

For early sowings which remain under

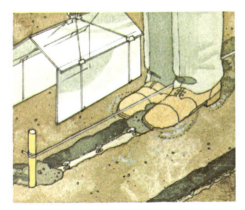

1. When the soil and air temperature are warm enough, sow seeds in pairs, 15-22 cm (6-9″) apart in seed drills.

2. To keep pods from dragging on the ground, support plants with pea sticks or short lengths of bamboo.

3. While the plants are young, hoe to keep weed competition down, and also to keep soil surface broken up.

cloches for some time, it is best to use the big barn-type cloches, because the plants will need plenty of growing space before all danger of frost has passed. If the weather turns cold, cover the cloches with mats or sacking to give extra protection against frost.

Transplanting

French beans grow best when sown directly where they are to grow. However, for very early crops, and in cold districts, you can sow pairs of seeds in boxes or pots in the greenhouse, four to six weeks before the last expected frost date. Because French beans do not transplant well, and tend to stop growing once disturbed, it is best to sow them in peat pots which can be planted out without any disturbance to the roots. Another method is to sow the seeds in blocks of turf, which can then be planted out in late spring. Those sown under cloches may also be transplanted, but the more usual method is to remove the cloches when no further frosts are expected.

Care and cultivation

French beans will produce heavier crops when regularly hoed and watered. Watering is particularly important in dry weather, when the crop's growth is liable to be checked, and the flowers may not set. If the flowers wilt and droop, the insects cannot penetrate and pollination will not take place. When this happens, spray the plants with a fine misty spray every morning and evening until the flowers have set. This fine mist will not be sufficient to keep the soil moist; a thorough watering, directed at the plants' roots, will also be necessary in dry weather.

Regular hoeing not only keeps weeds under control, it also keeps the surface of the soil broken up. In prolonged dry spells, some soils, particularly if watered by hose, form a hard surface crust. This prevents water penetrating the soil, and it runs off the surface without reaching the plants' roots. Hoeing also creates a

1. If it is hot and dry when flowering occurs, spray plants daily with a fine mist of water to aid pollination.

2. A mulch of clean straw, moist peat or leaf litter conserves soil moisture and protects plants from early frosts.

3. When harvesting, cut the pods with scissors or secateurs; never pull the pods off, or you may damage the plant.

dust mulch, which helps conserve soil moisture. A mulch of clean straw or leaf litter has the same effect, provided the soil is thoroughly watered before the mulch is applied.

Small doses of liquid manure are beneficial. To make, soak a bag of manure in a tank of water until the liquid is the colour of weak tea. Take care when applying not to splash the foliage, because liquid manure of this kind is more concentrated than the liquid feeds sold especially for foliar feeding, and can burn the leaves.

Strictly speaking, the dwarf varieties do not need support. However, they tend to get weighed down by the pods, which then rest on the ground and become vulnerable to slug attacks. In wet weather, they will get covered with mud, too. As a precaution, support the plants by tying them to short lengths of bamboo, or else grow them through pea sticks. Occasionally, dwarf varieties will send out runners in an attempt to climb; cut these off as soon as you see them.

The climbing varieties need the support of tall rods or canes around which they will twine in the same way as runner beans (see RUNNER BEANS). Erect one rod or cane per plant; these should be about 1.8 m (6′) high after they have been pushed well into the ground. The framework will consist of a line of pairs of canes, straddling the axis of the row, not less than 45 cm (18″) apart at ground level. Alternatively, use twiggy branches for support, or large mesh netting. Earthing-up around the base of the plant, up to the first set of leaves, gives additional support to the stem, as well as encouraging extra root growth.

If you made late sowings, and plan to harvest right through autumn, give the plants cloche protection from mid-autumn onwards. Alternatively, a thick mulch of clean, dry straw, applied when frost threatens, will help protect the plants.

Greenhouse growing

If you have a heated greenhouse with an

Planting distances between French bean plants depends on when and where they are sown, and whether they are to be harvested over several weeks, or picked all at once, for drying and storing. Usually, they are planted in double rows, 30cm (1') apart, leaving 60-90 cm (2-3') between each set of double rows. This allows for easy access for cultivating and harvesting. Rows of haricots are usually planted much closer together, as they are harvested all at once.
Remember that climbing French beans can overshadow lower-growing vegetables, so site them carefully.

air temperature of 16 C (60 F) and a minimum soil temperature of 13 C (55 F), you can grow good crops of out-of-season French beans in the borders. Greenhouses which are glazed down to ground level are best, as the French beans need plenty of sunlight. You can also grow them in frames, but only if you live in a really warm and sunny area.

Sow the seeds in good quality seed compost, with enough heat, any time from late summer to late winter. Expect cropping from late autumn through to late spring or very early summer. For minimum root disturbance during trans-

planting, use peat pots or sow the seeds directly onto soil blocks. Once the first pair of true leaves are showing, transplant them into the border or frame. The soil should not be too rich, or the plants will make excessively leafy growth at the expense of pod formation. Ideally, soil which has been manured for a previous crop is best.

Space the plants 22 cm (9") apart, in single rows 30-37.5 cm (12-15") apart in frames and in double rows about 30 cm (1') apart in the borders. Climbing varieties grown in the borders will need support. Use strong garden twine, fixed vertically to two parallel, horizontal wires. The top wire can run under the roof, and the lower one should be about 15 cm (6") from the ground. Two plants will climb up the same string.

Cultivation is the same as for outside growing, but make sure the plants are kept growing in a reasonably moist atmosphere, otherwise red spider mite could become a major problem, and ensure that the glass is as clean as possible, to allow maximum light to reach the plants.

Harvesting

The beans are ready for picking from ten to twelve weeks after sowing, depending on weather conditions. Once the pods have started to form, check them daily, as they mature quickly. Most varieties are best when about 10 cm (4") long. Unless you are growing the crop specifically for the seeds (either green, as flageolets, or ripe and dried, as haricots) do not allow the ripe pods to remain on the plant. If you do, the seeds will grow larger, but the texture and flavour of the

pod itself will deteriorate. Secondly, the plant will concentrate its energy on the swelling seeds, at the expense of the pod production, and your crop will diminish accordingly. Daily picking will ensure that cropping continues for five weeks, or more.

When tested, pods ready for eating will snap cleanly in half, without any stringy fibres. The beans inside will be visible, but will not have expanded to their full size. Cut the pods from the plant with scissors or secateurs. You can also sever them with thumb and fingernails. Never try to pull the pods off; the plants are very shallow-rooted and you may pull the whole plant out of the ground. French beans are best eaten on the day of picking, because, although they are excellent for deep freezing, they do not otherwise store well. If you plan to shell the half-ripe beans, and eat them as flageolets, leave the pods on the plants until they are just beginning to turn colour. At this stage, the beans should be pale green. They can either be cooked fresh or dried for later use.

French beans are excellent subjects for growing in pots, either in the greenhouse, or out-of-doors in a warm, sunny spot. Remember that soil in pots dries out very quickly, so water frequently in warm weather. Otherwise, cultivation is the same as for outdoor-grown French beans.

Brian Furner

1. Harvest in mid-autumn, when pods are pale brown and beginning to split; if it is cold and wet, dig up plants and hang indoors to ripen fully.

2. Spread shelled beans on trays, and dry them in a well ventilated room.

3. When completely dry, store in glass jars with tight-fitting lids.

Haricots

The beans of some varieties, if left to ripen fully, can be dried and stored for winter use. In mid-autumn, when the pods are pale brown and beginning to split, the beans are ready for harvesting. Cut the plants down, shell the pods, and spread the brown or white beans out on clean paper or wooden trays to dry. The floor of a greenhouse is a suitable drying place, but any room which is light and airy will do.

Some autumns turn cold and rainy before the pods have fully ripened. If this happens, dig up the plants, and hang them upside down in a greenhouse or attic. The pods can then finish ripening under cover; once the pods are brittle, shell and dry the beans in the usual way.

Aftercare

When cropping is over, cut off any remaining growth above ground level. If it is healthy and free from insects, place it on the compost heap. Otherwise, burn all stems and foliage to minimize the spread of pests and diseases. As with all leguminous crops, French bean roots will increase the nitrogen content of the soil as they decay. This is particularly important if the following crops grown on the site are nitrogen-hungry, such as brassicas and potatoes.

Exhibition tips

There is no special cultivation required for growing exhibition French beans; if you follow normal cultivation procedures and your plants are growing well, you should have plenty of pods up to show standard. One useful hint: French beans, when quickly grown, sometimes look a bit pale. To prevent this, give a light dressing of nitro-chalk, at the rate of 60 g per sq m (2 oz per sq yd), when the young plants start forming true leaves.

Mid-spring sowings outdoors should give ripe beans for early to mid-summer shows, provided the weather has been reasonable. If you live in a particularly cold district, it is safer to sow in peat pots in a cold frame in mid-spring, and plant out at the beginning of early summer. For late summer or autumn shows, cover possible crop failures by sowing small successional batches, say, at fortnightly intervals, until mid-summer.

The judges will look for straight, fresh, tender pods without any bumpiness; keep this in mind when selecting the beans. Twenty four beans are usually required, but it is safer to pick about twice this number, so you will have plenty of reserves at the show bench. Never pull the pods off the plant; cut them with scissors. Completely ignore enormous pods, which are likely to be tough and fibrous; they will not gain you any points.

To keep your beans from looking tired and stale, pick them at the last possible moment before the show. Make sure your hands are clean, because it is difficult to wash off stains on the pods without destroying the bloom.

As soon as the pods have been collected, lay them out on damp, clean cloths, and then roll the cloths up into loose bundles. They can travel to the show like this, provided they will not remain in the bundles for more than two days. If there is a longer interval between picking and the show date, it is best to pack the beans dry. A couple of hours before staging the pods, immerse them in cold water to restore their crispness.

Beans look nicest when displayed in a circular pattern on a plate. The tails of the pods should face outwards, towards the edge of the dish.

Pests & Diseases

Bean beetle (Bruchid beetle): because this pest resembles a weevil in appearance, it is sometimes called, incorrectly, 'bean weevil'. The female lays her eggs on the growing seed pod, or else on seeds which have been dried and stored. Once the legless grubs hatch out, they bore into the seeds, and then bite a round, window-like hole beneath the skin surface; it is through this hole that the adult beetle eventually emerges.

Besides feeding on the seed, the holes that they make allow secondary infections, such as fungal and bacterial diseases, to enter. Millepedes and wireworms also find it easier to attack pods which have been initially damaged by bean beetle. Remove and burn any seeds or pods which are holed, or which contain living grubs. Because these pests are usually seed-carried, the best precaution is to be sure your seeds are from a reliable source.

Slugs: these familiar garden pests feed on a wide variety of plants. Active chiefly after dark, they attack leaves and pods, biting large holes in them. During the day, they hide away in dark, moist, cool places. Slugs are often found in decaying vegetable matter, and on soils which are rich in humus and moisture.

One method of destroying slugs is to trap them. Place wet sacks, or heaps of damp vegetable refuse, such as cabbage or lettuce leaves or orange peels, at the base of the bean plants. Inspect the traps daily and destroy any captured slugs.

Alternatively, control slugs with pellets containing metaldehyde or methiocarb.

Capsids: these are sucking insects whose attacks produce pin-prick holes in the leaves and occasionally distort the pods. They attack the growing point of the plant, resulting in stunting of the plant and, if very young, in completely killing it. Control them by spraying or dusting with derris plus pyrethrum, or dimethoate if an infestation is stubborn. Because capsids drop to the ground

Ministry of Agriculture

These leaves show the main symptom of halo blight: spots surrounded by yellow rings.

Ministry of Agriculture

Round, dark, sunken spots on bean pods are telltale signs of anthracnose infection.

when disturbed, remember to treat the soil around the plant as well. Since the damage does not usually show until after the capsids have gone, it is best to start spraying in late spring, when the capsids actually begin to feed, particularly if you had damage the previous year.

Bean aphis (black fly): this insect is most troublesome in late spring, when it completely smothers the growing points of beans. Plants infested with bean aphis stop growing, and the few pods which develop may be covered with a black, sticky substance. Control by spraying with bioresmethrin or liquid derris, or dust with derris powder, and repeat as necessary. Remove and burn infected tops of plants as soon as enough pods have formed.

Bean seed fly: these pests destroy the seeds and the seedlings of newly planted French beans. The pale, legless larvae are most active between late spring and mid-summer. They attack the plants below ground, where they feed on the seeds, roots and underground stems of seedlings.

Because they are more likely to appear on land which has been given manures rich in nitrates, avoid excessively rich nitrogenous fertilizers. A second precaution is to dust the drills with gamma HCH before sowing or planting out.

Red spider mite: this minute sucking insect pest occasionally attacks French beans, especially if grown in hot, dry conditions. Watch for the appearance of leaves heavily speckled greyish-brown or pale yellow, together with webbing and slow plant growth. If it occurs, spray with malathion and give additonal water and ventilation. Remember to allow the correct time interval between spraying and harvesting.

Halo blight: this is a seed-borne, bacterial disease which is encouraged by the unnecessary practice of soaking the beans before sowing. The main symptoms are small, transparent spots which are surrounded by a yellow ring. Eventually the spots dry up, and where many are present, so that they coalesce, the entire leaf will wither. Seedlings may be killed outright, and even older plants can wilt completely. The pods can also be infected with round, moisture-oozing spots. Remove and destroy diseased plants as soon as seen. The best precaution is to only use seeds from reliable sources; never sow seeds which are wrinkled or blistered or have yellow spots on them. The variety *The Prince* is resistant to the disease.

Anthracnose: this fungal disease is usually associated with cool, wet growing conditions. The main symptoms are dark brown elongated spots on the stems which result in the leaves withering. The pods can have small, round, sunken spots, reddish-brown in colour, and the seeds inside diseased pods will eventually develop brownish-black markings. A half-strength mixture of Bordeaux (230 g in 46 litres of water, or 2 lb in 10 gallons of water) sprayed onto the infected plants offers some measure

GUIDE TO FRENCH BEAN TROUBLES

Symptoms	Probable cause
Seed leaves mis-shapen; seedlings stunted; small holes under surface skin of beans	Bean beetle
Irregular holes in leaves, stems and pods; faint silvery trails	Slugs
Pinprick holes with brown edges in young leaves; growing points blind	Capsids
Plants, especially growing tips, covered in small black sucking insects	Bean aphis
Roots and underground stems tunnelled	Bean seed fly
Leaves speckled greyish brown or yellow; webbing present	Red spider mite
Small transparent spots with wide yellow rings around them, which later dry up; leaves withered	Halo blight
Dark brown spots on stems, reddish brown spots on pods	Anthracnose
Dark brown or reddish black spots on roots and base of stems; roots withered looking	Root rot
Fluffy grey mould on stems, leaves and pods	Botrytis
Leaves mottled dark green, light green and yellow; stunted plants, mis-shapen pods	Virus diseases

of control, but this spraying must stop when the plants begin to flower. The plants should be destroyed after cropping, and dwarf beans grown in a different place for several years. Because the disease is seed-borne, the best precaution against anthracnose is clean seed, obtained from a reliable source.

Root or foot rot: this fungal infection occurs most often on soils which are cold and badly drained. Roots growing in these conditions will be weakened, and thus will be more vulnerable to attack. Unfortunately, the symptoms of root rot are not visible above ground. If a plant is not growing well, and has yellow, wilted foliage for no apparent reason, gently pry the soil away from the main stem. If root rot is the cause, then dark brown or reddish discolourations will be seen on the roots and base of the stems, and the roots will be withered looking. The crop is likely to be greatly reduced. As with all seed-borne diseases, the best precaution is to obtain clean seed from a reliable source. Affected plants should be destroyed after any crop has been taken. Those only slightly affected may be induced to throw out fresh roots by mulching up and around the stems.

Botrytis: this fungal infection, commonly called 'grey mould', is usually associated with cold, wet growing conditions; seedlings are particularly vulnerable. As its common name implies, the main symptom is fluffy, grey mould appearing on the stems, leaves and, occasionally, pods.

Sufficient ventilation is important; if you sow your beans under glass, make sure the seedlings are not overcrowded. Thin them as soon as they are large enough to handle, and always remove and destroy weak or damaged plants. If there is an outbreak of botrytis, control by removing badly affected plant parts and spraying the rest with sulphur, or dusting with a fine spray of sulphur dust. Benomyl is also effective.

Virus: two diseases, common mosaic and yellow mosaic, occur on beans. The former produces dark and light green mottling, and distorted leaves. The plants are stunted and the crop reduced. Yellow mosaic produces yellow irregular patches on the green leaves, and the pods can be considerably mis-shapen. Common mosaic can be seed-borne; both are carried by greenfly. As with all virus diseases, there is no remedy, and infected plants should be destroyed. Do not save seed for future sowing.

Varieties

Dwarf

The Prince: early crops of long, tender dark green pods, which are nearly stringless and well-flavoured; heavy cropping and very popular variety.

Masterpiece: pods long, straight and tender, best when cooked young; early variety, but with continuous pickings, cropping extends six or seven weeks.

Chevrier Vert: heavy cropper with medium length, dark green pods; sliced, used for flageolets, or dried for haricot beans; virus and anthracnose-resistant.

Kinghorn Waxpod: excellent flavoured wax bean with 15 cm (6″) long, fleshy pods, pale yellow; can be cooked whole.

Flair: very early, with heavy crops of straight, 13 cm (5″) long stringless, fleshy pods; good for both early cropping and autumn cropping from late sowings.

Glamis: extra-hardy stringless beans, suitable for growing in cold or exposed positions; pods straight and fleshy.

Royalty (Purple-Podded): heavy cropper with stringless, full-flavoured purple pods which turn green when cooked; very good for cold or exposed areas.

Cyrus: new variety with round, very slender pods; heavy cropper; can be cooked whole.

Gold Crop: American variety, with straight, yellow stringless pods about 15 cm (6″) long; plants vigorous and disease-resistant.

Remus: new variety with pods carried above foliage; pods 25 cm (10″) long, straight, dark green and fibreless.

Climbing

Earliest of All: heavy cropper, with medium-sized pods; crops can be used fresh or dried as haricot beans for winter use; grows to about 1.5 m (5′).

Largo: long, straight, stringless pods; can be eaten fresh or dried and stored.

Violet Podded Stringless: heavy cropper with purple flowers and deep blue-violet pods which turn green when cooked; flavour good; pods tender and fleshy.

Blue Lake White-seeded: short, fleshy pods in clusters; particularly well-flavoured; heavy cropper; seeds can be dried for use as haricots.

Haricot

Granda: primarily used for drying, but can be eaten green if required.

Comtesse de Chambord: another dual purpose variety, good for slicing or drying; grows strongly, so good for suppressing weeds in a new garden; very slow to mature, so avoid late sowing.

Left to right: *Cyrus, Royalty, Gold Crop*

Largo

Leeks

Allium ampeloprasum porrum (fam. *Alliaceae*)
Hardy biennial, grown as an **annual.**
Sowing to harvesting time: 30–45 weeks.
Size: leaves up to 30 cm (1′) long; bulbs 7.5–15 cm (3–6″) long and up to 11 cm (4½″) in diameter ('pot' varieties), 15–30 cm (6–12″) long and 5 cm (2″) in diameter (long varieties).
Yield: 10–12 plants per 3 m (10′) row.

One of the finest vegetables, the leek is easy to grow, useful, and very versatile. The blanched, elongated bulb at the base of the leaves makes a tasty fresh vegetable, either on its own or in stews and casseroles. The rich green leaf tops are excellent for flavouring soups. Besides being tasty, leeks are also nutritious; they are rich in vitamin A.

A member of the onion family, leeks are much easier than onions to grow. They are very tolerant of soil conditions, growing in any soil which is not waterlogged, and, unlike onions, they are generally free from pests and diseases. Most varieties are perfectly hardy and can remain in the ground through winter weather until needed. You can, by sowing early under glass, have leeks for harvesting in autumn, but it is really during winter and early spring that they are most welcome. Other garden vegetables are scarce at this time, and those in the shops are expensive.

There are long and short varieties of leeks available; the short, or 'pot' leeks are very popular in the north of England and Scotland, where they are often grown for exhibition work. Pot leeks are thick and stumpy, rather than tall, and have circumferences of up to 37.5 cm (15″).

Of the long leeks, broad flag varieties (sometimes called London leeks) are not frost hardy, and should be lifted before heavy winter weather sets in.

Suitable site and soil
Although leeks are tolerant of a wide range of soil types, they grow best on a moist, light soil that has been heavily manured for a previous crop. Freshly manured soil is not suitable, because leeks grown in very rich soil will be tough and coarse, with too much leaf growth. If the soil is in need of organic matter, it is best to dig in well-rotted garden compost, leafmould or peat

SOWING AND THINNING

1. If the soil is deficient in potash, apply a potash-rich fertilizer to the soil before sowing is spring.

2. Sow the seeds thinly, about 100 seeds to the metre, in shallow drills; cover the seeds with fine sifted soil.

3. Thin the young leeks in two stages, to a final distance of 10 cm (4″) apart; use thinnings for salads.

mixed with hop manure just before planting. If the soil is deficient in potash, apply a fertilizer rich in potash (fertilizers used for tomatoes are suitable).

In crop rotation, leeks follow lettuce, cabbage or peas, but it is not a good idea to plant them immediately after lifting early potatoes though this is often done. This is because the soil will be too loose and disturbed, and leeks do best on a firm soil.

Apart from considerations, the choice of situation in the vegetable plot may be influenced by the fact that leeks are generally left in the ground to be dug up as required throughout the winter, and can remain in the ground for a year or more. If you use a strict rotation system, you should bear this in mind, unless you have reserved a plot for semi-permanent crops like asparagus or artichokes, and there is some free space for your leeks. Do not grow leeks in the same place year after year, or there will be an increased risk of pests and diseases.

Sowing

Sowing in winter under glass is necessary if you want leeks ready for summer and autumn exhibition, but for normal household consumption wait until early to mid-spring depending on weather, when they can be sown outdoors. They can either be sown in a seed-bed for transplanting the following summer, or sown in their permanent positions. If sown in a seed-bed, you have the additional bother of transplanting. Against this must be balanced the fact that if they are sown in their permanent position, they will take up a lot of space for a very long time before producing results.

Sow the seeds thinly (about 100 seeds to the metre) as germination is usually very good, in drills about 0.5 cm ($\frac{1}{4}$″) deep, and cover the seeds with fine sifted soil. If properly stored, the seeds will remain viable for four years so you can keep extra seeds for future use. After covering the seeds, firm the drills down and water if the soil is dry. Drills should

TRANSPLANTING

1. Transplant leeks in early to mid-summer, when they are about 20 cm (8″) high; do this in showery weather if possible.

2. Cut back the roots until they are 2.5 cm (1″) long; trim the leaf tips back slightly.

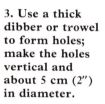

3. Use a thick dibber or trowel to form holes; make the holes vertical and about 5 cm (2″) in diameter.

4. Lower the young leeks into the hole and fill with water; the water will wash soil over the base of the plant, to keep it in position.

be 15 cm (6″) apart in the permanent bed. Germination should take 14–21 days, and thinning should begin as soon as possible, when the plants are not more than thin green shoots, about six weeks from sowing. Thin moderately the first time, as some of the plants may die, and then thin again, when all seems to be going well, so that the plants are about 10 cm (4″) apart.

Planting out

By mid-summer, when they are about as thick as pencils and 20 cm (8″) high, the leeks will be ready for transplanting to the permanent bed. If you can plant during showery weather, the young leeks will get over their planting check much more quickly; otherwise water the seedbed the day before lifting if the soil is dry. To eliminate the bother of sowing, thinning and transplanting, you can buy young leeks from your nurseryman at this stage. Leeks can stand the rigours of transport and once planted will quickly settle in.

There are several methods of planting out leeks, depending partly on soil type and partly on the quality sought. Exhibition leeks are usually grown on the flat, because it suits the special methods used for blanching and is least likely to damage the roots. Unlike those grown for kitchen use, leeks grown for exhibition should never have their roots or leaves cut back when transplanted. You can also grow leeks in shallow trenches, pot holes, or, if the soil is heavy and badly drained, on raised beds.

To plant leeks in holes, use a thick dibber or trowel; make the holes 15 cm (6″) deep, and 15–23 cm (6–9″) apart, depending on what size of leeks you plan to harvest. Many people prefer the taste of the smaller, tender, immature leeks to that of the enormous, prizewinning ones. Make sure the holes are vertical, and move the dibber about from side to side so that they are slightly larger at the top; the holes should be about 5 cm (2″) in diameter. Cut back the roots until they are 2.5 cm (1″) long, and trim the tips of the leaves back slightly. Place the young leeks into the holes so that they lean against one side, and gently fill the holes with water. The water will wash enough soil over the base of the plant for it to become established. As you hoe the rows from time to time, the holes will gradually fill up with soil. Leeks grown in this way will not be completely blanched, but the pale green portions seem to impart the best flavour to a soup. If you prefer thoroughly blanched leeks, this can be done quite easily by earthing up. A useful tip to note when planting is that by the time the leeks have reached transplanting size, it will be possible to see which way the leaves arch. They can then be planted so that the leaves of each plant run along the row and not at right angles to it. This takes up less space and reduces risk of injury during cultivation.

Another way of growing leeks is to plant them 25 cm (10″) apart in a trench. This method is particularly good if you have a deep, fertile soil; otherwise it is best to plant on the flat. The trench should be excavated to a depth of 30 cm (1′), and if there is more than one trench, they should be at least 75 cm (2′6″) apart. If you try to dig the trenches closer together, the walls of the trench are likely to collapse. Into the bottom of each

1. Dig trenches 30 cm (1′) deep and 75 cm (2′ 6″) apart; fork 7.5cm (3″) of garden compost into the bottom.

2. Cover compost with 15 cm (6″) of topsoil, and carefully plant leeks 25 cm (10″) apart; water thoroughly.

3. Grow quick catch crops, such as radishes or lettuce, on ridges, before soil is needed for earthing-up.

53

trench dig about 7.5 cm (3″) of well-rotted garden compost and cover it with about 15 cm (6″) of topsoil. Carefully plant the leeks, perfectly upright, in the bottom of the trench. Then water in as before. Form the remaining soil into flat-topped ridges between the rows. These ridges are excellent places for quick catch crops, such as lettuce or radishes, which will be harvested well before the soil is needed for earthing-up the growing leeks.

Cultivation and care

Water the young plants generously until they are well established. Soon after planting apply liquid manure. If the soil is not adequately rich in fertilizers, nitrate of soda, nitro-chalk or sulphate of ammonia may be applied at the rate of 10 g per metre run (1/3 oz per yard run) about five weeks after planting and watered in; alternatively, apply twice this amount of soot along the row when the plants are well established or liquid feed about once a fortnight through the growing season, instead of giving the single dressing of dry fertilizer.

Hoe between the rows regularly to keep down weeds and also to aerate the soil. Frequent hoeing also creates a dust mulch which helps conserve moisture.

BLANCHING
1. **To keep stems free of soil, place collars round stems up to the base of the leaves.**

2. **Then draw up soil from between rows, using a draw hoe; repeat as necessary, fitting another collar above the first one.**

3. **You can start blanching with paper collars; support paper collars with bamboo canes.**

4. **As the leeks grow on, replace paper collars with 10 × 30 cm (4 × 12″) clay drainpipes.**

Leaves which grow too long and unmanagable can be cut back slightly, so that they do not trail on the ground. Cut the long, dark green, outer leaves back by about 5 cm (2″) in early summer, again in mid-summer, and a third time, if necessary, in early autumn. If you are growing leeks for exhibition, however, do not shorten the leaves, unless they are decayed.

Blanching

Blanching leeks increases the proportion of plant which is edible, and improves the flavour, which would otherwise be strong and fairly harsh. Begin blanching in early mid-autumn; it is a gradual process and should be done in several stages, rather than all at once. There are several methods of blanching, depending on the way in which the leeks are growing.

If your leeks are growing in a trench, blanching consists of gradually filling the trench with soil to the bottom of the lowest leaves each time, until the plants have ceased to grow, which will probably be mid to late autumn, depending on the weather. This should give you 10–15 cm (4–6″) of blanched stem at least. One word of advice, however: the soil used for earthing-up must be dry, friable and very fine textured. If it is wet when earthed-up, rot is liable to set in. If the soil is lumpy, it will be difficult to handle and will not exclude light properly.

If grown on the flat, push the soil up around the plants, increasing the soil depth by about 5 cm (2″) each time. You can keep the stems free of soil by using collars, which are secured around the leeks up to the base of the leaves. Various materials can be used for the collar: lengths sawn from plastic piping, clay drain pipes, or, at virtually no cost, pieces of strong brown paper secured with string or rubber bands. If you use paper tubes, support them with bamboo canes. Whatever form of collar you use, the minimum diameter should be 7.5 cm (3″); they should be 30-37.5 cm (12-15″) long.

Leeks are very hardy, and can remain in the ground through winter weather until needed.

Attach the collars before carrying out the earthing-up process. As the plants grow, draw up more and more soil with a hoe, fitting another collar above the first one.

Although it is not strictly necessary, you can put planks of wood, on edge, along both sides of the row instead of using collars. This forms a sort of box into which the soil is put, until the desired height of soil is reached. With this system, you can use silver sand, leafmould or peat instead of soil.

Harvesting and aftercare

Leeks may be harvested from mid-autumn through to the end of late spring, depending on time of sowing and variety. The hardier varieties are left where they grow until needed. Never pull leeks out of the ground by brute force, or they will more than likely break in two, leaving you with a handful of leaves. Instead, lever them out of the ground with a spade or fork. Take the largest first; the smallest, if left until the spring, will put on some weight before running to flower. If the ground is likely to be frozen for long periods of time, it is a good idea to lift any leeks which are ready and store them in sand in a cool place, where they will keep for about a month. If, towards the end of the season, you have a few leeks still in the ground, but need the plot cleared for new planting, you can dig the leeks up and heel them in a shaded place, until needed. Lay them on their sides in shallow trench with the top part of the leaf stalk projecting above the ground, covering the rest of the stalk with soil. This also helps to stop them bolting.

You can, by leaving leeks in the ground and nipping out the flower stems, get a bonus crop: leek bulbs. These small white bulbs will form at the base of the plant; harvest them in early summer and use as onions or shallots.

If you grow prize-winning leeks and want to keep a particular strain for future show work, allow one or two leeks to flower. Tiny, complete plants, or 'pods', will form among the seeds on the seed pod; these can be detached and potted on in the greenhouse.

Exhibition tips

Leek-growing competitions, in which enormous size was the determining factor, have long been a tradition in the north of England and Scotland; today, well grown leeks can be an asset to any display, and perfect leeks are worth 20 points, the maximum for vegetables.

For mid-summer exhibits, seeds should be sown in early to mid-winter. Remember that with exhibition leeks, it is quality rather than quantity that is called for. Six is the usual number shown for single dishes, and nine leeks for collections, so do not get caught up in raising unnecessarily large numbers of leeks. Sow the seeds thinly in John Innes seed compost, so the tiny seedlings do not have to complete for food, air and moisture.

For germination to be successful, temperature should be kept at 13°C (55°F). After germination it can be reduced a little, gradually; remember that leeks are hardy and although they are required to be well-grown for early planting out, too much warmth will force them and make them leggy. When the seedlings are about 5 cm (2″) high, prick them out into pans filled with John Innes No 2 compost. The seedlings should be 7.5 cm (3″) apart in all directions. Be very careful not to damage the tiny single root which supplies nourishment to the plant until additional roots have formed. The young leeks will probably need potting again before planting out, into 12.5–15 cm (5 or 6″) pots. If small pots are full of roots some weeks before planting out

HEELING IN

1. Dig a narrow trench in a cool place; lay leeks on their sides with leaf stalks projecting above ground.

2. Cover leeks with soil and firm down with feet; heeling in helps to stop leeks from bolting.

Well-blanched specimens of Musselburgh, *a good variety both for exhibition and culinary use.*

time, then bigger pots will be essential. In early spring, put the trays in cold frames, to harden the young plants off before planting out in mid-spring.

Lifting the leeks prior to exhibition is a fairly delicate operation; it is all too easy to wreck a season's work by damaging the leeks at this time. Remember that as many roots as possible should remain intact on the plant.

Before actually digging them up, it is a wise precaution to gently tie the top foliage upright with soft twine. Well grown leeks tend to have brittle top foliage, and it will snap off if mishandled.

After tying the foliage, scrape away all sand, soil or peat from the base of the plant. Lift off any drainpipes; occasionally you may have to carefully break the drainpipe with a hammer to get the leek out. If they have been grown in cardboard tubes, it is best to leave the tubes on until the leeks have been lifted. The tubes are then cut open, carefully, with a sharp knife.

Lift the specimens with a fork, digging well under the roots so you do not inadvertently spear the leek. Once the leeks are out of the ground, wrap them in clean, damp cloths or paper; if you leave them exposed to the light, the blanched portions will rapidly turn green. Take them indoors and carefully cut away the first outer layer of soiled leaves. You may have to remove a second layer of leaves, but do not remove more than necessary, or the leeks' appearance will be damaged.

After removing the outer leaves, totally immerse the leeks in cold water, to get rid of all traces of soil. Change the water several times, until the leeks are perfectly clean. They should be cleaned while still tied, or the leaves may snap off in the water.

Leeks must be packed carefully for transport to the show; this is particularly important because their large size makes handling difficult.

Well grown pot leeks: these thick, stumpy leeks are very popular for exhibition work in the north of England. Pot leeks can be more than 30 cm (1′) in circumference, and are judged by their cubic size. Pot leeks for show must not be bulbous at the root end, but should be cylindrical in shape, and free from coarseness.

While in transit the leeks should be kept cool, otherwise the foliage will turn yellow.

Depending on the number shown, leeks are displayed flat on staging, in a basket, or vertically, like columns, on a specially built base. To display them vertically, make a round wooden base, about 2.5 cm (1″) thick, through which you hammer the required number of spikes. These spikes, usually bright metal nails, should be equi-distant from each other, and protrude about 5 cm (2″) above the board. Just·before the show, place the board right side up on the staging, cover the surface with a thick bed of parsley, and fix the leeks securely onto the nails. Because the leeks may tend to lean at slightly different angles, it is best to tie the tips of the leeks together with soft green twine. Three or four bands of twine should be enough to secure them firmly. When this is done, remove the twine which tied the individual leaves together, from the lifting stage onwards. If well done, the leeks will look like white columns, seemingly unsupported.

The judges will look for solid, thick leeks, not less than 30 cm (1′) long, without any tapering. There should no swelling at the base, or any discolouration. As with all vegetables, the leeks should be as uniform as possible.

Pests & Diseases

Leeks are relatively pest and disease free, as long as they are part of a crop rotation plan and are not grown on the same ground several years running.

Onion fly: Leeks are occasionally attacked by this pest, which is particularly troublesome in the larval stage, when the maggots tunnel into the plant tissue. The fly, which looks like a small grey house fly, lays its eggs in spring and early summer, near the base of the leek, on the leaves and in the soil nearby. Scattering diazinon granules in late spring will help to control the emerging larva. Like onions, young leeks seem particularly vulnerable. Lift and destroy and infested leeks; the main symptoms are yellowing and drooping foliage.

When lifting the infested leeks, make sure there are no maggots left lying on the ground. Because the flies are attracted to the smell of fresh manure, make sure leeks are not planted on freshly manured ground.

Leek moth: this small brown moth lays its eggs on the base of leek plants during mid and late spring. The emerging pale green caterpillars tunnel through the leaves, which are disfigured with white streaks. As more and more tunnels are made, the leeks loose their strength and may collapse and die.

The best method of control is a nicotine wash, applied first when the plants are still in the seed-bed, and again in mid to late summer.

White rot: this fungal infection attacks onions, shallots and garlic as well as leeks, and is most noticeable in hot, dry

Leek leaves damaged by caterpillars of the leek moth, which cause tattering and browning.

Pupae of the leek moth, in their cobwebby cocoons; the moths emerge in mid-summer.

summers. Plants grown in overcrowded conditions are particularly vulnerable. Infected leeks will have yellow leaves, with a white or grey fungus covering the underground base of the plant, looking like strands of white thread. The spores can remain viable in the soil for at least eight years, so proper crop rotation is the best precaution against white rot. Dusting the soil at sowing time with

---

GUIDE TO LEEK TROUBLES

Symptoms	Probable cause
Yellow, drooping foliage, tunnels in plant tissue	Onion fly
White streaks on leaves	Leek moth
Yellow leaves, white or grey fungus at base of plant	White rot
Leaf tips die back, white papery patches on leaves	White tip
Orange, powdery spots on older leaves	Leek rust

These orange, powdery spots indicate leek rust; infected leaves will turn yellow.

Musselburgh

calomel dust gives some additional measure of protection, and leeks grown on fertile, organically manured soil seem less vulnerable.

White tip: this is another fungal infection, which usually appears from late summer through the winter. Symptoms are a white die back of the leaf tips, white patches appearing on other parts of the leaf and stem, and stunted growth. Infected leaves look watery, thin and papery; eventually they rot away. Besides looking unpleasant, infected leeks wilt quickly and will not keep at all. Badly infected leeks should be removed and destroyed, and the remainder sprayed fortnightly with a copper fungicide until all white patches disappear.

Leek rust: this fungal infection is more prevalent when the autumn and winter are unusually mild. Leeks growing in soil which is rich in nitrogen but lacks potassium are particularly vulnerable. The symptoms of leek rust are orange, powdery spots on older leaves, which later turn yellow. Although they are disfigured, leeks with mild rust infections can still be eaten. Badly infected plants should be dug up and destroyed. To control the spread of the disease, spray the remainder of the leeks with zineb.

Varieties

Winter Crop: extra hardy variety, dark green foliage with large white stems; long lasting, keeps till mid-spring without loss of foliage.

Musselburgh: one of most popular varieties, crops very hardy and of good length, will tolerate wide range of growing conditions.

Early Market: early variety, excellent for autumn use; do not grow for late crops.

Malabar: quick growing variety for

Early Market

Malabar

Giant Winter

autumn use; stem medium length, with dark green tops.

Lyon Prizetaker: probably the most popular variety in cultivation; plants hardy and fine flavoured; stems long, thick and white.

Giant Winter (Royal Favourite): very large, pure white stems, leaves very dark; longest lasting, can be pulled in mid to late spring.

North Pole: new variety, late and very heavy cropping; vigorous growth and winter hardy.

Marble Pillar: early variety, suitable for

pulling from autumn through mid-spring; produces good, solid, very long white stems.

Northumberland: short, thick, early leek, to be pulled in autumn; original 'pot' leek of Northumberland miners.

Malines Winter: new variety; long, thick, heavy stems, dark green leaves; matures late.

Everest: exceptionally large leeks, perfect for table or exhibition.

Catalina: a new variety with long, thick, fleshy stems, mild flavour; very long standing, and can be left in the ground.

Lyon Prizetaker

North Pole

Peas

Pisum sativum (fam. *Leguminosae*)
Hardy annual
Sowing to harvesting time: 11-12 weeks for early
varieties; 12-13 weeks for second early varieties; 13-14
weeks for maincrop varieties.
Size: plants vary in height from 30 cm (1′) for the smallest
dwarf varieties to 1.8 m (6′) for the tallest plants. Pods
range from 7.5 cm (3″) to 15 cm (6″).
Yield: 40 plants per 3 m (10′) row, each bearing up to $\frac{1}{4}$ kg
($\frac{1}{2}$ lb) of peas.

Tender home-grown peas are one of the finest delights a gardener can enjoy. Once a treat for a few weeks in summer, with careful planning it is now possible to have a variety of fresh peas from late spring through to early autumn.

Peas have a very long history as a garden crop and many varieties have been evolved. There are early, second early and maincrop varieties, peas that climb almost two metres high and dwarf peas that need little support, the small-seeded and succulent petit pois, mangetout, or sugar peas, with edible pods, and purple-podded peas. All of these types can be grown successfully by the home gardener.

The varieties you choose to plant will depend on several factors. Peas need a great deal of space—tall more than dwarf and maincrops more than earlies—so consider how much space you have available. Decide if you like your peas very sweet, if you want to freeze or dry part of your crop, and for how long a period you want to harvest your peas.

Also, bear in mind that all peas are a crop for cool-temperate zones, as most varieties will stop producing pods when the temperature rises above 20 C (70 F).

Two types of seed

There are two types of pea seed, round and wrinkled. In the wrinkled, or marrowfat, varieties, some of the starch in the seed has turned to sugar. Although the seeds produce very sweet peas, they hold too much moisture for autumn sowing, and peas sown in autumn must be round-seeded varieties, several of which are hardy.

There are dwarf and tall varieties of both round and wrinkled seeds. In general, although there are some exceptions, early varieties of peas tend to be dwarf and the maincrop types taller and bushier.

Choosing a site

All peas need plenty of space. Choose an open, sunny site, but one sheltered from strong winds. Remember that the taller

1. Dipping seed in mixture
of paraffin and red lead.

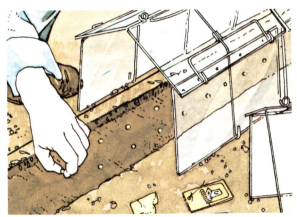

2. Sow first early varieties in double rows under
tall cloches. Put a mousetrap at each end.

3. Maincrop varieties can
be sown without protection.

4. Hoe around the seedlings to keep down weeds
and to prevent pea moths from laying eggs.

5. Remove weeds by hand
to avoid damaging the roots.

6. If the soil is very poor, apply a low-nitrogen
fertilizer when the plants are young.

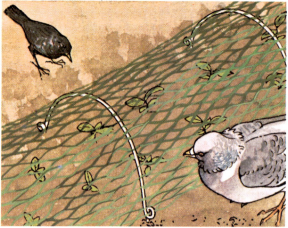

7. Water the seedlings often, especially in dry spells.

8. Protect young plants from birds with mesh net pea-guards, 12 cm (5″) high and 20 cm (8″) wide.

varieties will shade other crops growing alongside them, so plan your rows of crops with this in mind. Also keep in mind that the large spaces between the tall plants can be used for inter-cropping: quick-growing radishes or shade-loving spinach are both good.

Peas will grow well in a variety of soils, but you should take steps to provide for their special preferences. An acid soil is not very suitable, the ideal being a pH of 7.0. Carry out a soil test and correct any acidity by an application of lime the winter before sowing.

Peas like a rich soil, but not one recently enriched by applications of manure; it is better to sow them in soils which have been well manured early in the winter. Poor soils can benefit from chemical fertilizers containing superphosphate and potash, applied at the rate of 60 g per sq m (2 oz per sq yd) just before sowing. Use nitrogenous fertilizers very cautiously because the pea plant can extract nitrogen from the air for itself, and an excess of nitrogen leads to lush leaf growth at the expense of the pods. Peas need plenty of water and thrive in a reasonably heavy soil which retains moisture, although you must avoid waterlogging. The plants have penetrating roots, so dig the ground deeply and thoroughly.

Sowing the seed

Sow peas where they are to remain for their entire lives because they are deep-rooting and do not usually transplant satisfactorily. The roots must not be disturbed while the plants are growing.

Mice will eat pea seeds as fast as you sow them, so take some precautions. Many seed merchants sell seeds pre-treated with a proprietary mouse repel-lent, and these should be used if mice are a problem. If pre-treated seed is unavailable, another safeguard is to set traps at the end of a protective cloche or mesh net covering.

For all sowings, prepare a shallow drill 15-23 cm (6-9″) wide, and sow the seed 2.5 cm (1″) deep in rows 7.5 cm (3″) apart. Sow 6-10 seeds per 30 cm (1′). A good general rule is to allow a space between rows equal to the height of the fully grown plants. The peas should take between 10 and 20 days to germinate.

Spring-sown peas

Spring-sown peas are divided into three main groups: first early varieties, second earlies (also called early maincrop or mid-season varieties) and maincrops. The division is made according to the time that the varieties take to grow. If sown in early spring, first early varieties will produce peas ready to harvest in 11-

9. **Mulch with compost or strawy manure to retain moisture, feed plants and suppress weeds.**

10. **Use twiggy sticks to support growing dwarf peas.**

12 weeks. Second earlies sown at the same time will need 12-13 weeks, while maincrop varieties will require 13-14 weeks. It would be possible, therefore, to provide a succession of pickings by sowing varieties of all three groups at the same time. Alternatively, for a longer harvesting season, you can follow the usual practice and make a succession of sowings, starting with the earlies and proceeding to second earlies and then to maincrop. You can also gain time and produce a very early crop by protecting the first sowing of earlies from frost with cloches.

Autumn-sown peas

Some varieties of peas can be sown in early autumn to crop the following spring. For these early crops, choose hardy round-seeded dwarf varieties. In districts where the winters are mild, they can be sown in the open, but elsewhere they should be protected with cloches. Sow autumn peas more thickly than spring-sown crops, scattering them along the flat drill rather than planting each seed separately; this allows for some mortality. After a mild winter, autumn-sown peas should produce a crop several weeks earlier than those sown in early spring. A severe winter, however, may check them to such an extent that they

offer no advantage, producing at the same time as spring sown peas.

Care and cultivation

Peas are not an 'easy' crop, in that they do require frequent attention throughout their growing lives. Hoe regularly to remove weeds, but be careful not to damage the roots when pulling weeds close to the plants.

Peas need ample moisture, so water them frequently, especially during dry periods. Most of the diseases which infect peas are made worse in dry weather, so be on the lookout for any symptoms of trouble during a drought.

If the peas are sown in well-prepared, well-manured soil, then no additional feeding should be necessary during the growth period. In poorer soils the plants will benefit from an application of a compound fertilizer which is low on nitrogen and high on phosphates and potash. Apply this when the plants are young; use 30 g per metre run (1 oz per yard run). A mulch of garden compost, lawn trimmings, peat (unless the soil is acid) or well-rotted strawy manure will help to retain moisture. Apply this as near as possible to the base of the plants, where it will not only supply nutrients and retain moisture, but will also smother some of the weeds.

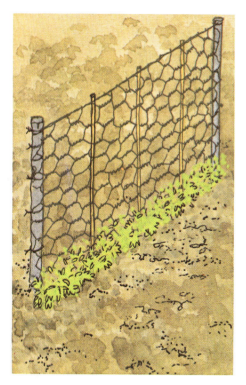

11. Make a supporting trellis for tall peas with a length of wire stretched between poles 1.5 m (5′) high.

12. If birds attack the young pods, drape fine fish netting over the plants and trellis to keep them away.

Staking the plants

Most dwarf and all tall varieties of peas require some staking. The plants grasp the support with their tendrils, so twiggy sticks or wire netting, both of which have plenty of tendril-holds, are the most useful. Unfortunately, traditional pea-sticks made from hazel wood thinnings are now very difficult to obtain and, therefore, expensive. Use conifer thinnings instead, or, for tall varieties, erect a supporting trellis of wire stretched between poles.

Stake the plants when they reach about 10-15 cm (4-6″) in height. Dwarf varieties need only small, twiggy sticks, one stick to each plant. Push the sticks a few inches into the ground close to the plants, but be careful not to damage the roots in the process.

Taller plants must be supported with stronger sticks, or with posts and netting. If you are lucky enough to get traditional pea-sticks or conifer thinnings, push these in the ground about 30 cm (1′) deep, one next to each plant. The stakes should stand about 1.5 m (5′) above ground.

If you decide to build a trellis, place hardwood poles at about 75 cm (2½′) intervals along the row. For a 3 m (10′) row, you will need five poles. Stretch a length of 1.5 m (5′) wide chicken wire or plastic-coated wire mesh along the row, and fasten it to the poles with wire. Make sure your poles are deep enough in the ground and your wire secure enough to withstand the wind.

When the pods begin to form, you can protect your crop from hungry birds by draping fish netting over the trellis.

A well-grown crop of dwarf variety early peas with full green pods ready for cutting.

Peas are ready for harvesting when the pods are full. Use scissors to harvest ripe pods as picking by hand can pull the plant out of the ground.

After picking clear the site. Remove any bits of pea haulm and save the wire for your next crop.

Harvesting the crop

Garden peas are at their best when fresh, young and green. Never let them become fully ripe and hard, as they will lose much of their flavour.

Peas are usually ready for harvesting about three weeks after flowering. Pick them when the pods have filled out and are firm to the touch. During a very dry summer some pods may not fill out completely, but if some of the peas are large pick them anyway before it is too late. Start picking at the bottom of the plant, and cut rather than pull off the pods. Check your plants frequently and harvest the pods regularly as they become ready. Some varieties may have a second, smaller crop after the main one, although these pods are less sweet and tender than the first.

Storing a crop

Peas should go into the kitchen as soon as possible after harvesting. However, if you have several plants and your crop is large you may want to dry and store some for winter use. Reserve a few plants for this purpose, and leave the pods to ripen thoroughly before picking. If the weather is damp, cut the plants and hang them upside down in a dry, airy place to finish ripening. Then shell the peas and dry them completely on fine wire, or mesh, racks before storing them in sacks

or jars in a cool, dry place. If you want to freeze some of your crop, pick the peas when they are at their best and prepare them quickly to retain taste and colour.

Aftercare

There is no point in trying to retain the plants after the pods have been removed. Clear the site and use it for another crop immediately; brassicas are a good choice. The pea haulm should be incorporated in the compost heap, unless there was a bad attack of pea moth. The roots, which are rich in nitrogen, can be left in the ground to benefit the following crop.

There are many different varieties of garden peas, including some very unusual ones. You might want to try one of these less common but delicious types.

Sugar peas or mangetout

There are a number of varieties of peas in which the pods are eaten whole with the peas still in them; the best known is the sugar pea, or mangetout. These plants vary in height from dwarf to tall, 30 cm-1.5 m (1-5′), and they are all heavy croppers.

Sow the seed in late spring in a sunny place, and then follow the cultivation instructions given for other varieties. Sugar peas always need staking, and they must always be protected from birds,

DRYING METHOD FOR PEAS

If you want to dry some peas, cut the plants with pods still on and hang them upside-down until fully ripened.

which for some reason find them particularly attractive.

Harvest sugar peas when they are young and tender, usually in mid to late summer, before the peas have developed in the pods. If you can feel the peas developing, you are too late. Pick and take them straight into the kitchen to enjoy them steamed or stir-fried at their fullest flavour. Older pods make a delicious soup.

Petit pois

Petit pois produce an abundance of small, sweet, delicately-flavoured peas; for flavour they are one of the finest vegetables. The plants are very hardy and grow to about 1 m (3′) tall, making them suitable for a small garden.

Sow the seeds in mid-spring, spacing about 15 cm (6″) apart in rows 1 m (3′) apart. These plants require the same care

as other varieties. They also need a great deal of water, so never let them dry out. Harvest the pods as soon as they have filled out in mid-summer. Cook them whole, as the peas will fall out of the pods then they are ready to be served.

Purple-podded peas

Purple-podded peas are attractive, tall plants with purple pods and green foliage. They can reach a height of 2 m (6′), and they are hearty and vigorous croppers on most soils. Because of their height, they require a lot of space.

Sow in mid-spring, and follow the cultivation instructions for other varieties. Purple-podded peas crop for an unusually long time, so allow for several pickings from mid-summer. Harvest when young, and shell and cook the peas (which are green, not purple) as you would for maincrop varieties.

Exhibition tips

Growing the fifty perfectly-matched pods required for exhibition demands a great deal of skill. If you want to exhibit your peas, choose a heavy-cropping maincrop variety with large, pointed pods. Sow and cultivate as you would for maincrop peas for the kitchen, and take extra care to keep the crop well watered and free from pests. When the pods begin to form, remove any that are weak or misshapen to give the exhibition pods more space to grow. In very hot weather, it is a good idea to shade the plants with cloth draped over the supports to prevent the pods from drying in the sun.

On the day of the exhibition, cut the fullest and best-coloured pods at the last minute, handling them as little as possible to avoid damaging the bloom. Hold them up to a strong light to make sure that they are well-filled and free of maggots, and then pack them carefully between layers of cotton wool. At the exhibition hall, arrange the pods on a plate in a wheel formation, with the stalks pointing inwards. The judges will look for large, green, well-filled and well-matched pods.

Pests & Diseases

Always take precautions to protect your peas from pests, otherwise you are likely to end up with a disappointing yield. Rotation of crops is an important factor in avoiding pea diseases.

Birds Birds are troublesome pests in the early stages, as they attack and devour the pea seedlings. Protect the plants with cloches or with pea-guards, half-cylinders of small-mesh wire netting; these can be home-made or bought from garden centres. Any deterrent you find effective will do: try a traditional scarecrow, entanglements of black cotton placed over the plants, polythene bags hung from stakes, or even twiggy sticks placed flat on the ground.

Mice Many inexperienced gardeners sow good seed in well-prepared soil, and still end up with less than half a pea crop. The culprits are mice, who eat the germinating seed and can quickly clear a row. Seed can be purchased from most merchants already dressed with mouse-repellant. If this is unavailable, another precaution is to dress the pea seeds with a repellent or poisonous substance before sowing. Paraffin and red lead are the traditional dressing with which the seed is coated. Special care should be taken, however, as the red lead *is* poisonous, especially to children.

Maggots from the pea moth can burrow into the pods and ruin the peas.

G. E. Hyde

Greyish-brown mould on the leaves is caused by downy mildew.

Ministry of Agriculture Fisheries and Food Crown Copyright

Pea moth This is particularly troublesome to maincrops; earlies are rarely attacked. The moths are active in summer, when they lay their eggs on the developing pea pods, or on the stems and leaves. The larva, which look like maggots with white bodies and black heads, bore through the pods and into the seeds, producing unusable 'maggotty' peas. Spray with derris or fenitrothion about 7-10 days before flowering to kill the maggots just after they hatch but before they can burrow into the pods. Spray very thoroughly, as peas will be destroyed if the maggots get into the pods where the insecticide cannot reach them. If pea moth is a serious problem in your area, stop growing maincrops and concentrate on the early varieties, which mature before the moth is ready to lay eggs.

GUIDE TO PEA PROBLEMS	
Symptom	*Probable cause*
Maggots in pods or peas	Pea moth
Holes around edges of leaves	Pea weevil
Silvery patches on pods or leaves	Pea thrips
Small holes or maggots in seed	Pea beetle
Powdery white patches on leaves	Powdery mildew
Greyish brown mould on leaves	Downy mildew
Rotting roots or stems	Foot rot fungus; Black rot fungus
Brown patches on leaves or pods	Leaf spot Fungus
Pale green or yellow patches on leaves	Mosaic virus disease

Regular holes around the leaf edge are typical pea weevil damage.

Mottled green and yellow foliage is caused by mosaic virus disease.

Pea weevil Both the adult and the larva of the pea weevil may attack plants. The 0.5 cm ($\frac{1}{4}$") long grey adults feed on the leaves, making regularly-notched holes around the edges. The females lay eggs in late spring in the soil around the plants, and the white, grub-like larva hatch out and feed on the roots. Hoe around the plants in late spring to stop the adults from laying eggs, and control the weevils with a spraying of derris at the same time.

Pea thrips Pea thrips can be a serious problem in very dry weather. They feed on the flowers, stems and pods, distorting the pods and reducing the crop. They are most numerous in late spring and early summer, when they lay their eggs on the pods. The orange grubs hatch out and feed first on the flowers and then on the pods and leaves, causing silvery, mottled patches which later turn brown. Treat the plants just after the flowers have set with a spraying of derris or resmethrin. As with pea moth, early varieties are infrequently attacked, so if thrips are a problem grow earlies instead of maincrops.

Pea beetle Pea beetles, or seed beetles, are a large family of insects which feed mainly on the seed of peas and other legumes. The adult beetles lay eggs on the dried seed, and the larva hatch out and burrow into the seed, leaving a small, round hole. Infected seed will not germinate, or it will germinate poorly. Clean seed purchased from a reputable seedsman should be fumigated and free of pea beetle grubs. If you discover living grubs, burn the infected seed.

Mildew Powdery mildew appears as white, powdery patches on leaves and pods. Maincrop varieties are most often affected, particularly in dry weather. Prevent by spraying the young plants with dinocap. Also, clear out any old haulms left from early plants, as these can spread the disease.

Downy mildew appears much less frequently, and it is only severe in very wet weather. It looks like greyish-brown mould on the underside of the leaves. Try zineb for bad attacks; otherwise destroy individual affected plants.

Other fungus diseases Peas are subject to occasional attacks but fortunately they are neither very common nor very serious. Foot rot and black rot both cause blackened, rotting patches on the roots and at the base to the stems. Plants grown in good soil as part of a rotation system are rarely affected. Leaf spot fungus disease produces tan-brown patches on the leaves and pods. Dig up and burn any fungus-infected plants as soon as you see them.

Mosaic virus disease Pea plants which have mottled pale green or yellow patches on the leaves and pods are probably suffering from a mosaic virus disease. Although not serious, it can cause distorted pods, so pull out and burn any diseased plants you see.

Varieties

There are numerous varieties of peas available to the home gardener, each with different advantages. Many gardeners tend to stick to old and tried favourites, but seedsmen are constantly working on breeding better strains. Study your seed catalogue carefully before deciding what to plant, and give special consideration to those available at your local garden centre, as they are probably those most suited to your area. We list here some of the most popular and widely available varieties.

Early Onward

Early varieties

Feltham First: round-seeded; very early, dwarf; excellent for sowing in late autumn or early spring for very early crops; heavy crop of well-flavoured peas.
Early Onward: very popular round-seeded type; grows to about 60 cm (2') high; useful for successional sowings; very good type for freezing.
Kelvedon Wonder: one of the earliest of the wrinkle-seeded types; good for successional sowing; heavy cropper of very sweet peas; reaches about 45 cm (1½') in height.
Kelvedon Triumph: a good variety to choose if growing for exhibition; dwarf; heavy cropper.
Kelvedon Viscount: suitable for autumn or early spring sowing; heavy and reliable cropper; very hardy plant.
Little Marvel: dwarf variety; crops well; particularly good in cooler areas.
Meteor: round-seeded variety for autumn or spring sowing; heavy cropping dwarf plants.

Second early varieties

Hurst's Green Shaft: a new variety; heavy cropper; pods borne in pairs at top of plant, resistant to downy mildew.
Superb: good variety for exhibition; produces large, curved pods; round-seeded dwarf type.
Lincoln: popular variety for its heavy crops of very sweet peas; produces small, dark-green pods; freezes well.

Meteor

Dark-skinned Perfection: medium-sized but well-filled pods; very sweet peas; plants reach about 1 m (3') tall.
Purple-podded pea: usually treated as a second early variety; small purple pods have excellently-flavoured green peas; grows to about 1.5 m (5').

Maincrop varieties

Greensleeves (Achievement): superb choice for table or exhibition, produces 15 cm (6") long, well-filled pods; very heavy cropper; vigorous grower.
Dwarf Greensleeves: enjoys all the advantages of *Greensleeves*, but small enough for the small garden.
Alderman: extensively grown tall variety; long, thick pods with large, well-flavoured peas; high yield.
Onward: one of the most popular and

Dark-skinned Perfection

Dwarf Greensleeves

Gloriosa

Oregon Sugar Pod

consistently reliable varieties: extremely heavy cropper of well-filled pods; dwarf plants; good for freezing.

Rentpayer: one of the smallest growing maincrop types; crops heavily with large pods.

Gloriosa: new type which has proved extremely reliable under all conditions; heavy cropper; excellent for drying or freezing.

Lord Chancellor: old variety, but still a reliable heavy cropper; produces long, well-filled pods; height about 1 m (3′).

Senator: grows to about 1 m (3′) tall, heavy cropper of medium-sized pods; peas of outstanding flavour which freeze well.

Trio: new multi-podded variety; good sized peas with an extra high sugar content. Excellent for freezing. The plants grow to about 30 cm (1′) high.

Sugar peas

Sugar Dwarf Sweet Green: one of the smallest mangetout at 45 cm (1½′); exceptionally heavy cropper of sweet, pale green pods.

Sugar Dwarf de Grace: reaches 1-1.3 m (3-4′) in height; early cropper; produces pods 7.5 cm (3″) long.

Oregon Sugar Pea: maximum yield; pods of high quality and flavour.

Petit Pois

Gullivert: attractive plants produce a high yield of small pods; delicately flavoured peas.

Cobri: dwarf plants reaching about 60 cm (2′), heavy cropper of very small, sweet peas.

Runner Beans

Phaseolus coccineus (fam. *Leguminosae*)
Perennial cultivated as **half hardy annual**
Sowing to harvesting time: 10-14 weeks
Size: This depends largely on the variety used, but normally they are picked when 15-30 cm (6"-12") long. Exhibition varieties may attain 60 cm (24") in length. Plants 2-3 m (6'-10') high; dwarf varieties 30-38 cm (12"-15")
Yield: 0.75-1 kg (1½-2 lb) per plant, or 5 kg (10 lb) per metre run

Reliable and easy to grow, the runner bean is often known as the 'amateur's vegetable'. Its ornamental scarlet or white flowers and succulent green pods have made it a firm favourite. Runner beans are perennial plants in their South American homeland, but in cool temperate areas they are grown as annuals from seed to avoid their susceptibility to frost.

As part of a good rotation plan, runner beans should follow brassicas or potatoes. Like other members of the family *Leguminosae*, runner beans possess root bacteria which convert nitrogen gas from the air to nitrogen compounds, thus enriching the soil for a following crop.

Selecting a site

Runner beans do best in a site that is both open and sheltered. Windswept sites and low-lying frost pockets are not suitable, because in windy or cold weather pollinating insects do not visit the flowers. Avoid siting your beans near any gaps in fences or hedges through which frost might enter.

When deciding where to plant your runner beans, remember they grow very densely, and a row of climbing beans will make a solid wall of foliage 2 m (6') high. This will shade adjacent rows of vegetables on either side for several hours a day, even if the bean rows run from north to south. Site them accordingly, perhaps at the end of a plot, or next to a wall.

Preparing the soil

The ideal soil for runner beans is a rich, loamy one, well supplied with moisture. Provided that the upper layers are well drained, the more moisture the better; good bean crops are dependant on adequate water. Avoid heavy clay soil as it is generally much too cold at sowing time; very shallow or sandy soils are not suitable as they tend to dry out in summer.

Well before planting time, dig your bean trench. This should be 30 cm (1')

1. Prepare trench well before sowing; double dig and incorporate manure.

2. Two weeks before sowing, apply superphosphate and potash.

3. Rake in the fertilizers, and level off the bed.

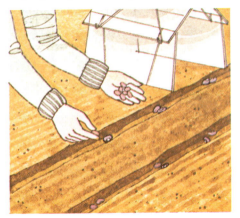

4. Sow in drills under cloches for early sowings, or in cold areas.

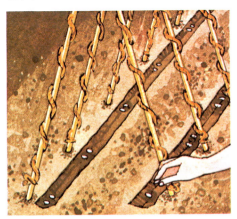

5. Position canes and twine; sow in deep drills, two seeds per cane.

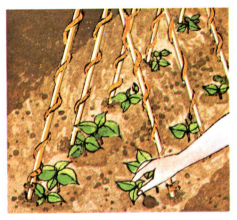

6. As seedlings start to grow, cut or pull out the weaker of the two.

7. Weed around young plants taking care not to damage them.

8. As plants wind themselves up the framework, tie in any stray growth.

9. When plants have reached the top of supports, pinch out growing point to encourage lateral growth.

10. When watering, soak the ground completely to reach the deeper roots. A light sprinkling is simply harmful.

11. Mulch over wet soil in early summer, to preserve soil moisture.

12. Keep picking regularly. Discard yellow, gouty pods—they are too old.

deep and a minimum of 60 cm (2') wide. On soil with a high clay content, deeper digging to a depth of 45 cm (1½') will help improve drainage.

It is very important to dig organic matter into the bottom spit, or spade depth, of the trench to help keep the soil open, friable, and moist; it will also serve as a source of nourishment for the growing plants. Well rotted manure or garden compost, at the rate of a litre (2 gallon) bucketful per sq m (sq yd) is sufficient; dig it in during the winter, to allow time for the soil to settle before spring sowing.

When preparing the soil, one point to remember is that too much nitrogen in the soil is sometimes a cause of bean flowers failing to be successfully fertilized, or 'set'. This is best prevented by avoiding fresh manure or artificial fertilizers known to have a high nitrogen content. As a precaution, 45 g (1½ oz) of superphosphate and 15 g (½ oz) of sulphate of potash per sq m (sq yd) applied to the ground immediately prior to planting will balance the presence of too much nitrogen.

Soil in industrial areas or towns is often prone to acidity; beans crop poorly on soil which is too acid. The ideal pH for this vegetable is between 6.0 and 7.0. Test your soil; if it is less than 6.0 add hydrated lime at the rates suggested in the soil test kit.

To train as bushes, pinch out growing point, then growing tips of laterals.

Sowing

Allow five or six plants per person; if you wish to freeze surplus crop allow double that amount.

Runner bean seeds are usually sown outdoors in late spring to provide a crop from mid-summer to mid-autumn. In especially warm and sheltered areas, however, it is possible to sow outdoors during mid-spring, to give a crop starting in early summer. Because the plants are tender and susceptible to frost, and because the seeds will not germinate unless the soil has warmed up, glass protection is needed for earlier sowings. This initial protection is particularly necessary if you live in cold districts such as the north of England.

Glass shelter for the young plants can be cloches, or a greenhouse or cold frame in which the seedlings can be raised in boxes. They can then be hardened off and planted out after all danger of frost has passed. Runner beans can also be raised in pots; peat pots are useful because you won't disturb the roots at planting out time. If you decide to use peat pots, remember to thoroughly wet the pots at planting out time; otherwise the dry pot will impede the flow of moisture from the soil to the plant's root system.

The rate of germination of runner beans is usually very high (80% or more) but it is still wise to sow a few extra seeds at one end of the row, so you will have a few replacement seedlings if there are failures in the row caused by poor germination or by pest damage to the germinating seedlings.

For planting, draw out a 5 cm (2") deep drill, water it, and sow two seeds every 30 cm (1') in either one or two lines depending on the method of support. If you are growing the beans up a single row of poles, sow one line only. If you are going to support the plants with pairs of crossed beanpoles, sow the seeds opposite each other in a double row 30 cm (1') apart. If you are going to use netting, sow two rows, again 30 cm (1') apart, with the seeds staggered. If you are

Fix netting to posts placed at 2 m (6′) intervals, sunk 45 cm (18″) into ground.

Rows of canes linked by wires, with stout poles and guy ropes either end.

planting more than one double row of runner beans, they should be at least 1.5 m (5′) apart.

If you plan to train the bean plants as bushes, plant the seeds 23 cm (9″) apart, leaving 60 cm (2′) between rows.

As soon as germination has taken place, earth up round the plants to protect them from possible frost damage. If they do suffer frost damage, pull them out. If it is not too late, make a replacement sowing, because frost-damaged runner beans will never fully recover. Stake the young plants as soon as possible to protect them from wind.

Methods of support
Whatever method of support you use, it must be absolutely rigid. One heavy cropping plant can weigh up to 2 kg (4 lb) and a whole row of them will be enormously heavy. A 3 m (10′) row of beans 2 m (6½′) high will have a surface

area of about 6 sq m (7 sq yd) of dense foliage. This is extremely vulnerable to strong wind; once a row of beans has collapsed, it cannot be re-erected. It will smother neighbouring rows of vegetables, and must be removed at once.

The simplest method of support is to give each plant one cane, or pole, pushing it 45 cm (1½′) into the ground, with 2 m (6½′) above ground. If you have access to a woody area, you can cut your own hazel, ash or sweet chestnut bean poles; alternatively, 2.4 m (8′) long bamboo canes, with a 3.7 cm (1½″) diameter at the thick end, may be used. Each cane is then linked to the next by thin wire or strong twine. At both ends of the row, two much stouter poles are inserted. Lateral stability is provided by straining wires from these heavy end poles to pegs driven into the ground, in the same way as guy ropes are used when

Growing in a tub: use a central pole and twine hooked to edge of tub.

Wigwam of bamboo poles, tied at the top, twine twisted around poles.

putting up a tent. If the row is very long, you may need intermediary posts and struts halfway along the row. Permanent clothes posts or nearby trees can be used to secure the end posts.

Another common method of support is to use the bean poles in pairs; they are inserted into the ground at an angle, so that the tops cross each other at a height of about 1.6 m (5½'). The poles are tied together at the crotch; after a row of these pairs of poles has been erected, 30 cm (1') apart, more poles are laid horizontally in the crotches, overlapping, and securely tied to the intersecting vertical poles where they meet (see figure 8). These horizontal poles help keep the framework rigid. If you are using bamboo canes, it is a good idea to twine string up the length of the smooth canes, to give the climbing bean vines something to cling to.

A third method is to grow the beans up netting, supported between strong posts. Use 10 cm (4″) mesh wire, plastic coated wire, or plastic netting. Posts supporting the netting should be 2.4 m (8′) long, hammered 45 cm (1′ 6″) into the ground at each end of the row, and at 1.8 m (6′) intervals along the row. Two internal struts are required for each post, to take the weight; these struts reach 90 cm (3′) up each pole and are well buried in the ground (see diagram).

If you are only growing a very small number of beans, wigwams of 6 or 7 poles planted in a circle and tied together at the top will suffice. The plants may be a bit crowded at the top, but will otherwise grow well. Runner beans can also be grown in a large tub, with strings tied to the top of a central pole, and radiating out to hooks which have been fixed to the tub (see diagram). A tripod with three canes is an alternate method of supporting beans grown in a tub.

Bush or dwarf varieties, when available, do not need support and are ideal for growing under cloches.

Eric Crichton

When the first vines start to search for something to climb, tie them loosely with raffia or string to their own poles. This is very important; once the beans have begun twining round each other for lack of proper training it will be impossible to disentangle them. Most people give each plant a pole, stick or string; some growers, however, allow up to four plants to use the same support. Choose the method you prefer.

Once the beans have started climbing up the supports, there is no training necessary until the tips reach the tops of the supports. Then pinch off the growing points. This encourages the production of lateral shoots further down the plant, and helps to increase crop yield.

Bush plants

Some gardeners train climbing runner beans as bush plants. This is done by pinching out the growing points at the first joint as soon as the young plants begin to run. When the plants are 30 cm (1′) high, nip off the growing tips of the lateral runners to promote bushy growth. You must continue removing these tips at weekly intervals for the plants to remain compact.

These are different from true dwarf runner beans, which grow naturally in a bush form about 45 cm (18″) high, and are cultivated as dwarf French beans. Unfortunately, true dwarf runner beans are not always available, as the strains tend to gradually revert to the normal climbing habit. When the seedgrowers' stock has deteriorated in this way, he must find a new source for true dwarfing plants.

Care and development
The main requirements of the growing runner bean plant are simple enough: moisture, weeding and feeding. The crop will not be successful if the plants are allowed to get at all dry. During spells of dry weather, water the plants at least twice a week. You must use enough water to soak the ground completely and reach down to the lowest roots. Light sprinklings are actually harmful, as they encourage the deep feeding roots to come to the surface, where they are vulnerable to hot sun and drying winds. If you are growing your beans in tubs, water them daily during droughts, as soil in tubs or pots dries out very quickly.

In dry conditions, mulching is helpful, as it slows the rate at which water evaporates from the soil. Lawn mowings, 5 cm (2″) deep, are often used as a bean mulch; bark fibre, if you can obtain it, is a particularly good mulch because water and liquid feeds can penetrate to the soil below. Apply mulch in early summer, making sure the soil to be mulched is moist.

Liquid feeding can be occasionally incorporated into the watering pattern as soon as the plants are flowering. Use soot water, alternating with a dilute liquid feeding made by soaking a bag of manure in a tank of water until the fluid is the colour of weak tea.

While the seedlings are developing, you must weed regularly. Hoe the weeds while they are still small, taking care not to harm the delicate roots and stems of the young beans. Once the beans are growing well, they cast a heavy shade which keeps down most weeds; hand weed as necessary. Mulching the plants also helps smother any weeds which might develop.

Failure of the flowers to set is sometimes due to hot, dry weather conditions. When this happens, the flowers wilt and insects and moisture cannot penetrate. Spraying the beans with a fine misty spray every morning and evening, under and over the foliage, during heatwaves may help. Plants grown on moisture-retaining soil should not suffer too badly in a drought.

Harvesting the crop
Runner beans will be ready for picking in mid to late summer, and the golden rule is to keep picking. You must look over plants every few days during the harvesting season, and pick off all young tender pods. Length is not a reliable guide to ripeness, as the length at which they are ready to be picked depends on the variety. In general, beans which have grown too long have coarse-textured, pale pods, and the beans inside are swollen and stand out like gouty finger joints. These are inedible and should be discarded. Be careful to remove all old, stringy beans which have been overlooked under the dense, leafy growth; as long as these remain on the plant, further bean production is reduced.

Remember to remove slug-damaged, badly twisted or muddy pods as well, as they reduce the cropping potential of the plant and may invite infection. Pick the beans early in the morning or evening if the weather is hot. If you don't use them right away, store them in a cool larder, where they will keep for a couple of days, or in a refrigerator, where they will keep a bit longer. The best solution is to either freeze the surplus beans, if the variety is suitable, or share them with friends or neighbours.

At the end of the season, when clearing the plants after final harvest, leave their tuberous roots in the ground. They are rich in nitrogen and will improve the soil for a following crop.

Exhibition tips
If you want to grow beans for exhibition purposes, you will be losing some of the total crop weight the plant would have otherwise produced, as you must remove all pods competing with the few grown for exhibition.

Among the varieties particularly suited to exhibiting are Scarlet Emperor, Yardstick and White Achievement.

Treat the plants normally until you have pinched them out two leaves above the last flower truss when they have reached the top of the bean poles. Then stop all laterals two leaves above a flower truss. Three weeks before the show date, begin feeding your plants regularly with liquid manure. About a fortnight before the show, select the most promising of the pods, marking them with a bit of string. Then thin the trusses to two or three pods, supporting the weight of the beans by tying them in lightly to the poles or netting. Remember to remove the other beans from the plant, so they don't absorb nourishment intended for the show pods. Some exhibitors run their fingers down the show pods, as they are developing, exerting slight pressure on the beans as they do so. This stretches the pods and keeps them from being bumpy or 'beany'.

The length of the beans exhibited depends on the variety, but they should be from 38-50 cm (15-20″) long and 2.5 cm (1″) wide. Besides length, the judges will consider the beans' colour and texture. A top quality pod will be young, fresh and crisp, without any bumpiness from swelling seeds.

An exhibition dish of runner beans usually contains 24 pods, as alike as possible. If some beans reach their prime condition a few days before the show, cut them off, leaving 2.5 cm (1″) of stalk on the pods. Store them stalk downward, until the show, in a jam jar containing 1 cm ($\frac{1}{2}$″) of water which is changed daily.

On the day of the exhibition, choose your best pods and lay them neatly and as straight as possible on a large plate or across the bench.

Some exhibitors save home-grown seed from year to year. This is a dangerous practice, because of the high risk of seed-carried infections. Halo blight, anthracnose, bean beetle or root rot will effectively end any hope of prize winning.

Varieties

Runner beans have been divided into early and maincrop varieties, according to their time of harvest. Separately listed are some stringless varieties which are now being offered. There is no list of dwarf runner beans because the availability of these varieties fluctuates from one year to the next, due to deterioration of the seed stock. If you intend to freeze any surplus runner beans, make sure you select a suitable variety.

Early varieties

Zebra: attractive mottled pods 23 cm (9″) long; heavy cropper with aromatic flavour, suitable for freezing.

Scarlet Emperor: popular variety, ideal for general garden use; can be grown on poles or as a bush bean, suitable for kitchen and exhibition work; pods 30 cm (1′) long; not suitable for freezing.

Kelvedon Marvel: can be sown under cloches from mid-spring for exceptionally early crops; best results obtained by growing as a bush bean without poles; pods 25-30 cm (10″-12″) long; suitable for freezing.

Sunset: pale pink flowers, heavy cropper; can be grown up supports or as bush beans; if grown in bush form it will produce an early pick of pods; pods 30 cm (1′) long; not suitable for freezing.

Yardstick: pods up to 60 cm (24″) long;

Scarlet Emperor

Brian Furner

heavy cropper, exceptionally straight pods; excellent for exhibition work; suitable for freezing.

Maincrop varieties

White Achievement: white seeded, white flowered general purpose runner bean; kitchen or exhibition quality; pods 45 cm (1'6") long; not suitable for freezing.
Crusader: very heavy cropper; pods 40-50 cm (16"-20") long; suitable for freezing.
Enorma: heavy cropper; pods up to 52 cm (21") long; suitable for freezing.
Goliath (Prizetaker): pods up to 60 cm (24") long; heavy, reliable, and uniform crop; suitable for freezing.
Streamline: pods up to 45 cm (18") long; scarlet seeded; not suitable for freezing; good flavour.

Stringless varieties

Desiree: very heavy cropper (averaging 40 pods per plant); completely stringless pods 25-30 cm (10"-12") long; good performance under dry weather conditions: suitable for freezing.
Fry: white seeded, white flowers; pods 35 cm (14") long; good cropper during hot, dry weather; suitable for freezing.
Red Knight: heavy and early cropper; very good flavour; has pretty red flowers; pods 30 cm (1') long; sets well in hot, dry conditions; freezes well.

Brian Furner

Desiree

Pests & Diseases

Runner beans are relatively trouble free, but may be affected by any of the following:
Halo blight: this is a seed-borne disease which is encouraged by the unnecessary practice of soaking the beans before sowing. It takes the form of small, yellow transparent spots which are surrounded by a yellow ring. Eventually the spots congeal and dry up and the whole leaf withers. Seedlings may be killed outright, and older plants wilt completely. Diseased plants should be removed and destroyed as soon as seen. The best precaution is to only use seeds from reliable sources: never sow seeds which are wrinkled or blistered or have yellow spots on them.
Bean beetle (Bruchid beetle): these are frequently, though incorrectly, known as 'bean weevils' because of their visual similarity to true weevils. The eggs of this beetle are laid on the growing seed pod, or else on seeds which have been dried and stored. After hatching, the legless and curved grubs enter the seed and bite a round hole beneath the surface skin of the seed; this appears as a little window through which the adult beetle finally emerges. The damage done by these pests is twofold: because the growing grub feeds on the seed, the amount of nourishment for the seedling is diminished, if the germinating seedling is not killed outright. Secondly, the holes made by the beetles allow such other pests as millepedes and wireworms to enter, and expose the seed to attacks by fungal and bacterial growths. Any seeds found to contain living grubs or beetles should be burned; they should *never* be placed on the compost heap or left lying about. Because these pests are seed carried, you must be absolutely certain that your seeds are from a reliable source.
Slugs: one of the most familiar of all creatures which attack plants, they feed chiefly after dark, both above and below ground. They will attack the leaves,

Damaged and distorted runner bean leaves: the effects of capsid bugs.

An infestation of black bean aphis, commonly known as black fly, on a runner bean shoot.

stems, roots and pods.

During the day they hide away in dark, moist, cool places. Their favourite haunts are decaying vegetable matter, moist, heavy, sour soils or even alkaline soils which are rich in humus and moisture.

It is very difficult to eradicate slugs in heavily infested areas. Because slugs have the ability to cast off poisons or irritants which may fall upon them by excreting slime, to be effective you should always repeat an application of slug pellets on successive nights. Alternatively, use powdered lime and powdered copper sulphate mixed together in equal parts and forked into the soil at the rate of 30 g (1 oz) per sq m (yd). This will kill the slugs, but overuse of copper sulphate may harm the soil, so apply carefully and sparingly.

Another method of destroying slugs is to set traps at the base of the affected bean plants. These traps may be wet sacks, or heaps of damp vegetable refuse, such as lettuce or cabbage leaves or orange peels. It is most important that the traps are inspected daily and the captured slugs destroyed.

Capsid bugs: these are sucking insects which distort the leaves and mark the pods, occasionally attacking the growing point of the plant. They can be controlled by spraying or dusting with nicotine or derris plus pyrethrum. Because capsids drop to the ground when disturbed, remember to treat the soil around the plant as well.

Botrytis: this is a fungus always present in the atmosphere which appears on the plants as a fluffy grey mould. The fungus usually occurs in cold, wet, weather conditions, and is encouraged by humid, still air. Seedlings are particularly vulnerable and may collapse and die.

Sufficient ventilation is important; if you sow your bean seeds under glass make sure the seedlings are not over-crowded, and any damaged plants removed and destroyed. Botrytis can be controlled by dusting with a fine spray of sulphur dust or spraying with colloidal sulphur.

Bean aphis: this is a black aphis which completely smothers the growing points of beans in late spring. The affected plants stop growing, and the few pods which develop are covered with a black, sticky substance. It can be controlled by spraying with liquid derris or dusting with derris powder, repeated as necessary. The infected tops of plants can be removed as soon as enough pods are formed.

Bean anthracnose: this disease is sometimes called 'blight', 'rust' or 'canker', and thrives in damp, wet conditions. The symptoms are black spots which soon grow into sunken, circular pits surrounded by red lines. Leaves, stems, and pods may be affected. The disease penetrates the pods and infects the seeds,

Symptoms of bean mosaic: yellowish areas spreading among the dark green of the leaf.

Later stages of halo blight: the transparent ringed spots dry up and leaf begins to wither.

which then develop brownish-black markings. A half-strength mixture of Bordeaux (230 g in 46 litres of water, or $\frac{1}{2}$ lb in 10 gallons of water) sprayed on the infected plants helps control anthracnose, but this spraying must stop when the plants begin to flower. A seed-carried disease, the best precaution against anthracnose is clean seed.

Root rot: this occurs most often on soils which are cold and badly drained; the roots are weakened and made liable to attack from soil fungi. When this happens, dark brown or black spots can be seen on the roots and stems, just below the soil level. As with all seed-borne diseases, the best precaution is to obtain seed from a reliable source.

Bean mosaic: this disease, sometimes called streak, leaf roll, or yellow edge, is caused by a virus which infects the sap. Its symptoms are yellowish-green areas showing among the darker green areas of the rest of the leaf. External applications are not very effective in controlling mosaic, and badly infected plants should be dug up and destroyed. Because this disease is carried by sucking insects, especially aphids, a good precaution against mosaic is to spray the plants with derris or malathion. Because the virus can also be carried on gardening tools, any secateurs, hoes, etc, which have come in contact with infected plants should be thoroughly cleaned in a strong antiseptic solution.

GUIDE TO RUNNER BEAN TROUBLES

Symptom	Probable cause
Small transparent spots with wide yellow ring around them which congeal and dry up; infects pods, stems and leaves	Halo blight
Seed leaves misshapen, seedlings stunted, small holes under surface skin of bean; may be gaps in row	Bean beetle
Pinprick holes with brown edges in young leaves, leaves later tattered, growing points blind	Capsid bug
Fluffy grey mould on leaves, stems and pods; plants rot off at soil level	Botrytis
Irregular holes in leaves, stems and pods; faint silvery trails	Slugs
Sunken black spots, edged in red, on leaves, stems and pods	Bean anthracnose
Plants covered in small, black, sucking insects	Bean aphis

Spinach

Spinacea oleracea (fam. *Chenopodociaceae*), winter, prickly (seeded) or long-standing prickly spinach
Spinacea oleracea inermis, summer or round-seeded spinach
Tetragonia expansa (fam. *Aizoaceae*) New Zealand spinach
Hardy or **half-hardy annual**
Size: height to 20 cm (8″); width 30-37.5 cm (12-15″) for summer and winter spinach; trailing, width to 90 cm (3′) for New Zealand spinach
Sowing to harvesting time: 6-8 weeks
Yield: 150 g (5 oz) per plant before it bolts for summer type; 240 g (8 oz) per plant for winter type; 360 g (12 oz) per plant for New Zealand spinach

Spinach is a highly nutritious vegetable, rich in protein and vitamin A. It is quick growing and needs a minimum of care; by successional sowings and giving some winter protection, you can have good crops of spinach all year round.

There is some confusion over the name 'spinach' because it is used for many vegetables which are not true spinach but have leaves which are eaten like those of spinach. For example, 'perpetual spinach' or 'spinach beet' is a member of the beet family. Here we are dealing with the cultivation of three types: winter, summer and New Zealand.

True spinach is winter, or prickly spinach. 'Prickly' refers not to the leaves, but the seed capsule. It is a spreading, branching plant, with triangular dark green leaves. At one time winter spinach was thought to be hardier than summer spinach. This has been disproved,

however, and round seeded varieties can be sown right through the year.

Summer, or round spinach is a variety of winter spinach; it has round smooth seed capsules and slightly larger lighter green leaves. Summer spinach has a bad reputation for bolting, or running to seed. When this happens, the plants send up tall leafy stems with small green flowers at the top; the leaves then become bitter tasting and unpleasant to eat. Premature bolting is easily controlled, however, by making quite sure that you meet the basic cultivation requirements. Spinach must never run short of water, and needs some form of shade during the hottest summer months. Equally important is thinning the seedlings as soon as possible so they are never overcrowded. Spinach grown in crowded, starved conditions is more liable to bolt.

Spinach is an excellent, nutritious vegetable, relatively quick and easy to grow.

One sowing of summer spinach will give about three weeks picking; to get continuous supplies, you should sow at three-weekly intervals. Because winter spinach is less likely to bolt, two or three sowings in late summer through mid-autumn should give supplies right through winter and into early spring.

New Zealand spinach is not a true spinach, although it tastes fairly similar. It is not as hardy as winter or summer spinach, and is most successful in hot dry summers. Because it does well in very sunny conditions and does not bolt, it can be planted where ordinary spinach would do poorly. New Zealand spinach is a vigorous spreading plant, with floppy stem and fleshy, arrow-shaped leaves up to 12 cm (5″) long.

Suitable site and soil

To grow year-round supplies of spinach, you must make several successional sowings. The conditions needed for successful growing will change according to the time of year and variety of spinach grown. A warm, sheltered site is required for winter spinach and early sowings of summer spinach. From late spring through mid-summer, however, too much warmth and sunshine may lead to bolting, so a cool shady site is preferable. Spinach is ideal for growing in the shade of peas or beans during hot summer months.

New Zealand spinach needs a light, well-drained soil in a hot sunny position, and will crop well where ordinary spinach would quickly run to seed. New

87

1. Start sowing under cloches in late winter; continue successional sowing until mid-summer.

2. For free draining soil, make a shallow trench 30 cm (1') wide, with a central drill 2.5 cm (1") deep.

3. Thin the seedlings when they are 2.5-5 cm (1-2") high, to a distance of 12.5-15 cm (5-6") apart.

4. Shallow hoeing keeps weeds down and also creates a dust mulch which helps conserve moisture.

Zealand spinach likes soil fairly rich in lime, so it does particularly well on chalk or limestone subsoils; avoid acid soils or lime them well before growing, at a rate determined by the result of a soil test.

The needs of spinach vary throughout the year, so it is difficult to work spinach into a rotational cropping plan. Because it is such a quick grower, however, spinach is an excellent catch crop and can be grown and harvested without interfering with slower-growing crops, such as leeks or cabbages.

Spinach needs a rich moisture retentive soil, and it is a waste of time to sow on a dry, poorly worked site. The ground should be well dug over and watered, using between 5 and 10 kg per sq m (12 and 22 lb per sq yd) of rotted manure or garden compost; the high rate is best if the soil is light or sandy. At the same time a dressing of fertilizer containing 12% nitrogen and 6% each of of phosphate and potassium should be worked in at the rate of 30 g per sq m (1 oz per sq yd). No further feeding should be needed.

Sowing

Besides sowing frequently, you must sow spinach in large enough quantities to provide reasonable supplies for your

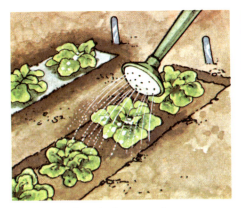

5. Water often in hot weather; use a fine spray or rose on your watering can so soil is not washed away.

6. Spinach is good for intercropping, and will grow well in the shade of runner beans or peas.

7. When harvesting, take only a few leaves from each plant at one time; overpicking can kill the plant.

8. After the final harvest, chop up the plants and dig them into the soil to act as green manure.

family. Whereas 'little and often' applies to the sowing of radishes and lettuce, it does not entirely apply to spinach. A whole panful of leaves when cooked will boil down to a couple of spoonfuls; if you then overpick to get enough leaves, the plants will stop producing new leaves and may die altogether. A good rule of thumb is to allow five plants per person per sowing, or a half metre (20″) row per person. 30 g (1 oz) of seed is enough to sow 3.6 m (12′). If you have more seed than you need, you can either share it with friends or store it; properly stored spinach seeds will keep for five years.

Make the first sowings under cloches in late winter, and continue making successional sowings at the rate of one every three weeks until mid-summer. It is best to use bolt-resistant varieties for these early sowings.

If your soil is light and very free draining, you can reduce the problem of drying out and bolting by making a shallow trench in which to sow the seeds. For each row of seeds, hollow out a trench 5 cm (2″) deep and about 30 cm (1′) wide. In the middle of this tench, make a drill another 2.5 cm (1″) deep to sow the seeds in. This shallow trenching system will allow you to flood the trenches, with little water loss. If the soil

1. Sow from mid-summer through to mid-autumn. For heavy soils, make small ridges on which to sow seeds.

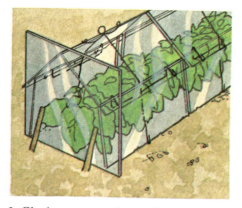

2. Protect open grown spinach from winter weather with a layer of bracken or clean straw.

3. Cloches are an alternative way to protect winter spinach; cloches also helps keep the leaves free of mud.

is very dry, water it thoroughly just before sowing, or soak the seeds in water for a few hours prior to sowing. If you are sowing more than one row of spinach, make the rows at least 45 cm (1½′) apart. You can grow good spinach with a spacing of 30 cm (1′) between rows, but the extra width allows you to cultivate the plants and harvest them without trampling on the bottom leaves. For some of the larger varieties, such as *Sigmaleaf* or *Greenmarket*, 60 cm (2′) between rows would be better, and for New Zealand spinach 90 cm (3′) is needed.

Germination may be sparse, so it is best to sow one seed every 7.5 cm (3″) and thin later. The seeds are actually capsules containing two or three tiny seeds, so you may get two or three seedlings at each station. After sowing, cover the capsules with 2.5 cm (1″) of soil, and press down firmly with the back of a rake. Germination should take place one to two weeks after sowing.

Winter spinach should be sown from mid-summer through to mid-autumn, at the same spacing and depth as for summer spinach. However, with winter spinach you have to avoid too much water rather than too little. If your soil is heavy, it is best to form small ridges on which to sow the seeds. Make them 7.5 cm (3″) high, with 60 cm (2′) from centre to centre. These raised ridges will help keep the spinach dry in the winter, which is important for a good crop.

Because New Zealand spinach is not quite hardy, it is best to sow in early spring in pots under glass and then plant them out in early summer, spaced 60 cm (2′) apart in all directions. You can sow them under cloches outdoors in mid-spring or in the open in late spring.

Before sowing, it is advisible to soak the seeds of New Zealand spinach for two or three hours in water to aid in germination as the seed coat is very hard. Whichever method of sowing you use, sow them in groups of threes, to allow for some failure in germination which may occur.

New Zealand spinach is an excellent crop for hot dry sites, as it is bolt resistant.

Cultivation

Thinning the young seedlings is very important; overcrowded plants are more liable to become diseased, unlikely to develop fully, and more likely to run to seed. Thin seedlings of summer spinach when they are 2.5-5 cm (1-2″) high, to a distance of 12.5-15 cm (5-6″) apart. Thin again when the leaves of adjacent plants begin to touch each other to a final spacing of 22-30 cm (9-12″) apart. If more than one seed germinates at a station, select the strongest and thin out the rest. Winter spinach being slightly smaller should be thinned to 22 cm (9″) apart; New Zealand spinach grows very large and needs to be spaced 90 cm (3′) apart in all directions.

Never let the soil dry out in hot weather, otherwise summer spinach is likely to bolt. Remember, though, that spinach needs a steady, constant supply of moisture: overwatering after a long dry spell can also lead to bolting. Too much water in late summer can also lead to soft rank growth, easily frosted in the autumn. Make sure you use a fine spray or rose on your watering can to avoid washing any soil away.

Keep the beds weed free, although healthy growing spinach will form a dense, impenetrable ground cover leaving little room for weeds. If weeds do appear, either hand weed or hoe. Regular shallow hoeing also prevents the soil from caking in hot weather, and provides a dust mulch which helps conserve moisture.

Although New Zealand spinach will not bolt in hot dry weather, it needs a steady supply of water at such a time. Harvest growing tips frequently, so that the plant will produce a continuous supply of sideshoots.

Cloche protection is very useful if you want to continue picking through winter, and get an early spring crop as well. Winter spinach sown under cloches in early autumn will be ready for picking from late autumn on. Protecting with cloches also helps keep the leaves free of mud. If you have no cloches it is a good

1. New Zealand spinach thrives on limey soil; if your soil is acid, apply lime before sowing.

2. Because the seed coat is hard, soak the seeds in water for a couple of hours before sowing.

3. Sow in pots in early spring; plant out in early summer, spacing 60 (2') apart.

4. Harvest growing tips frequently, so the plants will produce a steady supply of sideshoots.

5. Picking usually starts from early summer onwards, five to six weeks after sowing, and continues until the first hard frosts of autumn. Cut the fleshy shoots with pointed leaves when they are about 22 cm (8") long.

idea to protect open grown spinach from late autumn onwards with a layer of bracken or clean straw placed between the rows. Polythene tunnels are also effective with an occasional airing on mild days, but watch for slugs.

As long as the soil is reasonably rich and has been well prepared, there is no need to apply additional fertilizers once the spinach has been planted. However, you can apply nitro-chalk in early spring, at the rate of 30 g per sq m (1 oz per sq yd) to help winter spinach make a bit more spring growth.

For all types of spinach, after you have finished harvesting, chop the plants up with a spade and dig them back into the soil; they will then be a kind of green manure and enrich the soil.

Harvesting

Winter, summer and New Zealand spinach are harvested in much the same way. The thinnings of spinach are eaten first. Dig these up whole and cut the roots off. Thinnings of summer spinach are very useful for salad, as they are tender, less bitter and less stringy then fully grown leaves. When the main plants are ready, take a few leaves off from each plant. Moderate picking encourages the formation of new leaves; too much picking will kill the plant. A good rule of thumb is to take off no more than half the leaves at any one picking. Select the largest and most fully formed leaves, but do not leave them until they are old and tough.

When you are picking spinach, try to take the leaves only, leaving the stem. If they are young leaves you should be able to nick them off between your finger and thumb. Otherwise, twist the midribs and pull them off outwards or cut them with scissors to avoid damaging the main stem.

Winter harvesting should start in late-autumn. Do not pick the plants as hard as summer spinach. Unfortunately, the thinnings are not suitable for salads, as they are stringy. Pick only the larger outside leaves, allowing the young leaves

to grow on. Light pickings will enable you to have a longer period of harvesting, until spring, when the first crops of summer spinach should be ready.

New Zealand spinach is slightly more difficult to harvest because the plants are larger and tend to sprawl all over the ground. However, if you keep removing the growing tips, the plants will produce an enormous amount of leafy growth from a small area.

Start picking the fleshy shoots with pointed leaves when they are about 22 cm (8") long. Picking usually starts from early summer onwards, five to six weeks after sowing, and continues until the first hard frosts of autumn. If you miss one or two of the tips, and the plant flowers, it may self-sow and appear again the following year, in mild areas.

Exhibition tips

The main problem with exhibiting spinach is that the leaves tend to go limp as soon as they are cut, and it is difficult to stage an attractive exhibit composed solely of wilted leaves. To help prevent wilting, cut the leaves as close to the ground as possible the night before the show, preferably in cool weather. The number of leaves required for an exhibit is 15-25. It is a good idea to pick two or three times this amount, so you can select the best. Wash the leaves under cool running water to remove any soil. Then place the stalks in a bucket or large jar of water and store in a cool place overnight. The next day, lay the selected leaves on a large plate, with all the stalks pointing towards the centre, like the spokes of a bicycle wheel. Spray the leaves with cool water and cover them with a light cloth until just before judging.

New Zealand spinach is a separate category, although the preparation is similar. After gathering, strip off all the old leaves, and display the remaining leaves in a basket. For both New Zealand and ordinary spinach, pale green or yellow leaves, or those which are small or broken, will be considered defective.

Varieties

Broad Leaved Prickly: long standing; large deep green leaves; good for autumn sowing.

Longstanding Winter (Prickly): best variety for winter use; deep green thick leaves; quick growing; slow to bolt.

Greenmarket: large, dark green leaves; slow to run to seed; winter hardy; very heavy yielding; any virus infection will have only minor affects.

Sigmaleaf: round seeded variety suitable for spring or autumn sowing; can stand for long period of time without running to seed.

New Zealand Spinach: soft thick fleshy leaves; trailing habit; withstands hot dry conditions.

Monnopa: low oxalic acid content; fine flavoured; bolt resistant; winter hardy; for autumn sowing.

Cleanleaf: emerald green leaf; leaves borne well above the soil so they are not splashed by mud.

King of Denmark: large, round thick-leaved summer variety.

Monarch Long Standing Supergreen: dark green, round summer variety suitable for freezing.

Long Standing Round: quick growing; dark leaf; good for spring sowing.

Brian Furner

Broad Leaved Prickly

Brian Furner

Greenmarket

Harry Smith Collection

New Zealand Spinach

Brian Furner

Longstanding Round

Pests & Diseases

Spinach blight: this disease is caused by the cucumber mosaic virus. It is a serious disease and any infected plants should be dug up and burned as soon as the symptoms are seen. Usually the first symptom is yellowing of the younger inner leaves, and later the older ones. The inner leaves then become puckered and/or small, the leaf margins roll up, and the leaves die. Because spinach blight can be transmitted by aphids, try to keep your garden free of these pests, and also weeds, which may be infected with the virus, and infested with greenfly. As with other viral infections, there is no absolute cure; the best precaution is to cultivate the plants properly and watch for any sign of the disease, removing any suspect plants as soon as they are seen.

Downy mildew: this fungal infection is most liable to occur where the spinach is grown in crowded or very wet, cool conditions. It spreads very quickly particularly in wet weather, and can rapidly ruin a crop. The symptoms are yellowish patches on the upper surfaces of the leaves and downy grey growth on the undersides. The best precaution is to avoid damp conditions and thin the young plants well. Pick off and destroy any infected leaves; if the attack is severe, spray the remainder with zineb or copper fungicide.

Leaf spot: the symptoms of leaf spot are small light brown spots on the leaves, each with a darker margin. Although they are only 6 mm ($\frac{1}{4}$") across, if the infection is bad the spots join up into large areas and destroy the entire leaf. As with many diseases, the weakest plants are the most susceptible, especially if growing in badly drained soil. Remove and burn infected leaves as soon as you see them, and spray the remainder with captan or zineb. Spray again a fortnight later.

Damping off: this fungal infection causes seedlings to collapse at ground level and then die. Because it occurs most frequently in close, wet conditions, the best precaution is to sow thinly and make sure the seedlings are not over-crowded or overwatered. Thiram or captan treated seeds will be well protected.

Magnesium deficiency: magnesium is one of the constituents of chlorophyll. If spinach is lacking magnesium, pale areas will appear between the leaf veins. Eventually the pale areas turn brown. The deficiency is most liable to occur in very acid soils, or where an excess of potash makes magnesium unavailable to plants. A good mulch of well-rotted garden compost should help with the problem, and heavy dressings of bulky organic matter when winter digging will gradually eliminate it. On very acid soils, apply lime also. Alternatively, if such

---

GUIDE TO SPINACH TROUBLES

Symptoms	*Probable causes*
Outer leaves wilt and die; inner leaves turn yellow, curl up and die	Spinach blight
Yellow patches on upper surfaces of leaves, downy grey growth on underside	Downy mildew
Seedlings collapse and die at ground level	Damping off
Pale areas between leaf veins	Magnesium deficiency
Yellow blotches on leaves, leaves curled	Manganese deficiency
Leaves turn brown, wither and die	Mangold fly
Seedlings die (New Zealand spinach)	Millepedes
Irregularly shaped holes in leaves, faint silvery trails	Slugs
Stunted distorted leaf growth	Aphids

These spinach leaves have been damaged by aphids, which feed on the sap.

The maggots of mangold fly damage leaves by feeding on them; leaves become blistered.

manures are not available, Dolomite or magnesium limestone can be applied in winter, at about 210 g per sq m (7 oz per sq yd).

Manganese deficiency: the disease called 'speckled yellows' which appears on beet, is really a symptom of manganese deficiency and can also affect spinach. Affected plants have leaves with yellow blotches between the veins, and the leaves tend to curl up, the trouble being most marked in mid-summer. Both very sandy and very alkaline soils can be deficient in manganese, also those which are fairly alkaline and contain a good deal of humus. Some natural

recovery can occur, but if not, foliar spraying with manganese sulphate at 2 oz in 5 gal water with a few drops of liquid detergent, will help the plants considerably.

Mangold flies: the maggots of the mangold fly damage the leaves of spinach by feeding on them to produce large blisters. They are most damaging in late spring when the plants are young; infested leaves turn brown, wither and die. Remove the worst affected leaves and spray the remainder in widespread attacks with trichlorphon as soon as the symptoms are seen; do not forget to allow the specified interval to elapse between treatment and harvesting so that all traces of poison are gone.

Millepedes: these pests are liable to cause problems on soils which are very damp or have a high humus content. New Zealand spinach seems to be the most vulnerable; millepedes feed on the roots of seedlings and young plants, but in general little trouble need be expected in a well worked soil. They are difficult to control; apply gamma-HCH if a severe infestation is apparent while preparing the soil for sowing.

Slugs: if the leaves have irregularly shaped holes in them, and there are faint silvery trails nearby, then slugs are the probable cause. They feed at night, and are most active in the spring and autumn. Thorough cultivation of the soil helps keep the slug population down. You can set traps of piles of decaying vegetable matter near the spinach. Inspect the traps daily and destroy any slugs you find. If the infestation is severe, use metaldehyde or methiocarb slug baits.

Aphids: the damage caused by these insects is twofold. They feed on the sap in the leaves, which results in stunted and distorted leaf growth. They also transmit viral diseases and the honeydew they leave on the plants encourages sooty mould. Handpick affected leaves, as soon as seen, and spray with derris, malathion or bioresmethrin if the infestation persists.